Writing Behind Eve

For students to become college-ready writers, they must be exposed to writing throughout the school day, not just in English class. This practical book shows teachers in all subject areas how to meet the Common Core and make writing come alive in the classroom. The author provides exciting ideas for teaching argument writing, informational writing, project-based writing, and writing with technology. Each chapter is filled with strategies, prompts, and rubrics you can use immediately.

Special Features:

- A variety of writing strategies that work in any subject area
- Rubrics for assessing writing, as well as ideas for having students create their own rubrics
- Samples of student work in different formats
- Ideas for teaching students to break the Google homepage habit and conduct effective research
- Cross-curricular writing assignments for science, history, ELA, electives, and PE
- Suggestions for teaching summary writing, an essential academic skill
- Ideas for staff professional development on Common Core writing

Heather Wolpert-Gawron is an award-winning middle school teacher and a popular blogger through Tweenteacher.com and Edutopia.org. Her first book, *'Tween Crayons and Curfews: Tips for Middle School Teachers*, was published by Eye On Education in 2011.

Dec 16
Jan 12   3-4
      20   5+6
Feb   24   7
m   9   8+9

Other Eye On Education Books Available from Routledge
(www.routledge.com/eyeoneducation)

Rebuilding Research Writing: Strategies for Sparking Informational Inquiry
Nanci Werner-Burke, Karin Knaus, and Amy Helt DeCamp

Common Core Reading Lessons: Pairing Literary and Nonfiction Texts to Promote Deeper Understanding
Stacey O'Reilly and Angie Stooksbury

Big Skills for the Common Core: Literacy Strategies for the 6–12 Classroom
Amy Benjamin and Michael Hugelmeyer

Teaching the Common Core Speaking and Listening Standards: Strategies and Digital Tools
Kristen Swanson

The Common Core Grammar Toolkit: Using Mentor Texts to Teach the Language Standards in Grades 3–5
Sean Ruday

Authentic Learning Experiences: A Real-World Approach to Project-Based Learning
Dayna Laur

Vocabulary Strategies That Work: Do This—Not That!
Lori G. Wilfong

Common Core Literacy Lesson Plans: Ready-to-Use Resources, K–5
Common Core Literacy Lesson Plans: Ready-to-Use Resources, 6–8
Common Core Literacy Lesson Plans: Ready-to-Use Resources, 9–12
Edited by Lauren Davis

Helping English Language Learners Meet the Common Core: Assessment and Instructional Strategies, K–12
Paul Boyd-Batstone

Teaching Students to Dig Deeper: The Common Core in Action
Ben Johnson

Writing Behind Every Door

Teaching Common Core Writing in the Content Areas

Heather Wolpert-Gawron

Routledge
Taylor & Francis Group

NEW YORK AND LONDON

First published 2014
by Routledge
711 Third Avenue, New York, NY 10017

and by Routledge
2 Park Square, Milton Park, Abingdon, Oxon OX14 4RN

Routledge is an imprint of the Taylor & Francis Group, an informa business

© 2014 Taylor & Francis

Library of Congress Cataloging-in-Publication Data
Wolpert-Gawron, Heather, author.
    Writing behind every door: teaching common core writing in the
    content areas/Heather Wolpert-Gawron.—First published 2014.
    p. cm.
    Includes bibliographical references.
    1. Language arts (Secondary)—Standards—United States—States.
    I. Title.
    LB1631.W587 2014
    428.0071′2—dc23
    2013034334

ISBN: 978-0-415-73464-6 (hbk)
ISBN: 978-0-415-73208-6 (pbk)
ISBN: 978-1-315-81986-0 (ebk)

Typeset in Bembo
by Florence Production Ltd, Stoodleigh, Devon

Printed and bound in the United States of America by Publishers Graphics,
LLC on sustainably sourced paper.

Contents

Acknowledgments   *viii*
Meet the Author   *ix*

Introduction   **1**

Prologue   1
What's In a Name?   2
The Importance of Transfer   4
A Little Educational History to Get the Ball Rolling   6
Writing as the Universal Subject   12
A Brief Note on the Need for Tweens and Teens to Write   18

**1   The Common Core Standards as a Meaningful Guide,
     Not an Instruction Manual**   **19**

*Welcoming Back an Old Friend: Project-Based Learning (or, in this case,
    Project-Based Writing)   20*
Brushing the Dust Off of the 6 Traits (+ 2)   25
Developing Meaningful Assessments and Prompts   27
Student-Created Assessments and Rubrics   31

2   Argument: The Universal Writing Genre   **35**

The Argument for Argument   35
Features of Argumentation as a Writing Genre   38
Possible Structures of Cross-Curricular Argumentation Essays   43
A Brief Note on Scoring Arguments   48
Cross-Curricular Assignments and Activities   50
    Science   51
    History   53
    ELA   54
    Electives   55
    PE   56

3   Informational: It's All Around Us   **59**
The TED Unit   60

[handwritten: Pick a Topic they]

[handwritten: next 1-12]
[handwritten: 230]
[handwritten: 3+4   pg 90]

Contents

Collaboration and Differentiation Can Co-Exist 61
Team Charter Template: Collaboration Constitution 63
Information Hunting: Breaking the Google Homepage Habit 67
Developing a Problem Statement 68
The Student-Created Resource Library 71
The Importance of Visualizing Data 73
*Uncommon Assessments to Show Informational Research
    (Even in a Narrative Unit)* 76

4 Narrative: There's a Place for it in All Disciplines   **80**

*The Infusion of Narrative Elements into Interdisciplinary
    Content* 80
Incorporating Informational Writing into a Narrative Unit 86

**5 Summary: Get to the Point! The Underrated
Writing Genre**   **91**

The Summary Card 92
Chunking Text 92
What's the Big Idea? 93
Cornell Notes 93
The Executive Summary 97
Scoring Summaries 103

6 The Multi-Genre Genre   **104**

The Case for Writing Desegregation 105
*The Ultimate Multi-Genre Writing Projects: Websites
    and Apps* 112

7 Techniques to Teach Writing That Work   **116**

The Big List of Writing Strategies to Use in Any Classroom 116
    Color-coding 116
    Strategies for Embedding Evidence 118
    Strategies for Incorporating Commentary 119
    Dual-Entry Journals 123
    Modeling 123
    Differentiated Writing Assignments 125
    Using a Writer's Notebook 125
    Blogging 127
    Accessible Scaffolds 128
    TTW—Think, Talk, Write 131
    Train Them to Be Teachers 132
    Teaching Academic Vocabulary 133
    Using Acronyms 134
    Using Flipbooks 137
    Providing a Classroom Library 138

Handwritten annotations: "Get To the point", "58 John", "Jan 20 in the Am 8:00-8:30"

8 Writing with Technology for the Common Core   143

Modeling to Create a Tech-Rich Classroom   146
Digital Learning Tips for Students   148
What Kind of Tech-Savvy Teacher Do You Want to Be?   150
Creating an Online Student Lounge   152
The Big List of Common Core Technology Resources   154

**9 21st Century Professional Development in Writing for
Every Teacher**   157

The Common Core Professional Learning Community   158
Developing a Universal Common Core Language as a Staff   159
Developing Site-Based Training in Writing Across the Disciplines   162
Quick and Efficient Tips to Score Writing   164
Developing an Online Common Core Themed Faculty Lounge   165
Get Thee to a Writing Project!   167

Appendix A: TED Persuasive/Memoir Unit   171

Appendix B: Student-Created Rubric   173

Appendix C: Oral Feedback Sheet   174

Appendix D: The Problem Statement   175

Appendix E: Narrative/Informational Writing Checklist   176

Appendix F: Writing Genre Matrix   178

Appendix G: The DARPA Project Checklist   179

Appendix H: Peer Review Packet   180

Appendix I: Hooks   181

Bibliography   *182*

Acknowledgments

To all of my writing teachers:

To my first grade teacher, Mrs. Valentine, who taught me that periods don't go at the ends of lines; they go at the ends of thoughts.

To my second grade teacher, Mrs. Douglas, who first mentioned the metaphorical hamburger paragraph format.

To both of my third grade teachers, Ms. Lydon and Ms. Fleming. One taught me that you could combine writing with numbers to tell a story about data, while the other taught me that memoir had voice.

To Mrs. Brownfield, Ms. Spindler, Mrs. Ashbrook, and Mr. Canon.

To Ms. Sauve who taught me to write lyrically, and to try to have fun writing, even while composing expository papers (not an easy task to ask a bunch of eighth graders).

To Mrs. Creasy what taught me how to write a thesis statement.

To my tenth grade teacher, Mrs. Dunn, who informed me that I write "too Rococo" and then gave me a dictionary to figure out what that meant.

To my twelfth grade Composition teacher, Mr. McCatty, in whose class I first experienced the power of sharing one's own writing in an author's chair.

To all the teachers of the National Writing Project from whom I continue to learn, year after year.

To Addie Holsing, who taught writing and comprehension using brain-based strategies and multiple intelligences before the terms had ever been invented.

To Elaine Keysor, Liz Harrington, and Kenna McRae, all of whom make me wish I was a student again, if only for the chance to be theirs.

To Suzie Menerey, whose daily generous sharing of originally created resources has helped to educate hundreds of students in many more classes beyond the walls of her own.

To my father, who was my first writing teacher and who remains a heck of an editor.

To my husband, who first encouraged me to blog, helping me leap from the antiquity of the quill pen to that new-fangled computer thing.

And to the amazing writing teachers in the classrooms of every school, be they English teachers, math teachers, science teachers, elective teachers, or PE teachers, who work to teach eloquent communication to students every day.

Meet the Author

Heather Wolpert-Gawron is an award-winning middle school teacher who also writes a popular education blog as Tweenteacher. She has authored workbooks on teaching Internet literacy for grades 3–8, workbooks on project-based writing, grades 3–8, as well as the upcoming *Nonfiction Reading Strategies for the Common Core, Grades 1–8*. She is also the author of *'Tween Crayons and Curfews: Tips for Middle School Teachers*, a book written for Eye On Education Publishing.

Heather blogs for The George Lucas Educational Foundation's Edutopia.org as well as the occasional post for The Huffington Post. She is a member of the Center for Teaching Quality's Teacher Leaders Network, a Fellow of the National Writing Project, and is devoted to helping teachers regain control of their profession through elevating their practice and educating themselves on policy. She is passionate about educational technology and blended learning, and she works to help tech-tentative teachers become more savvy online and off.

Heather is dedicated to a new educative movement, one that incorporates the most innovative and differentiated 21st-century classroom of today with the online learning strategies students will need for their tomorrows. She believes teachers have a vital role to play in K12 instructional design.

She is wife to Royce, whom she met in second grade, after karate-chopping him at recess. Additionally, she is mom to 7-year-old Benjamin and 3-year-old Samwise (yes, like the Hobbit) whom they call Sam. She lives with all her boys and their boxer/corgi mix, their laughter and chaos, in Los Angeles, CA.

2005 SS Curriculum adapted
6 Traits

Introduction

> The Standards insist that instruction in reading, writing, speaking, listening, and language be a shared responsibility within the school. The K–5 standards include expectations for reading, writing, speaking, listening, and language applicable to a range of subjects, including but not limited to ELA. The grades 6–12 standards are divided into two sections, one for ELA and the other for history/social studies, science, and technical subjects. This division reflects the unique, time-honored place of ELA teachers in developing students' literacy skills while at the same time recognizing that teachers in other areas must have a role in this development as well.
>
> (Common Core Standards)

Prologue—June 2012

It's amazing what a few months can do. In 2010, I published my first book, *'Tween Crayons and Curfews: Tips for Middle School Teachers*. It was a book sharing strategies on building community and lesson design for an age group that struggles to find meaning in school because they are, at that time in their lives, struggling to find meaning in themselves. I focused on project-based learning and evolving one's practice through reflection. Since then, the educational world has been turned on its head with the imminent arrival of the Common Core Standards and their corresponding assessments.

But upon reading the Common Core Standards, I realized that the strategies many of us already use apply to this new generation of expectations. However, I have a number of colleagues, both online and offline, who are nervous about this change, and I got to thinking "why?"

Why are great teachers nervous about this standards-based shift? I realized that what's different about the Common Core Standards is that one of the biggest changes it demands is the use of an under-utilized muscle. The muscle of teaching writing.

For teaching a subject is very much like going to a gym. With every lesson and unit and year that you teach a particular content, your muscle to instruct students in those topics becomes stronger. That's why it can be so deflating as a teacher to be bumped from one subject to the next, year in and year out. You never get the chance to really pump up your brawn. However, the converse is also true. Every year you neglect a strategy, the ability to teach with it deeply gets farther and farther away.

For ELA teachers, the upcoming shift is subtle. It's a change in percentages, and not all of them we agree with. Narrative is downgraded yet still present. Informational and argumentation have now become universal. So here's the rub. How do we ELA teachers become enthused and educated in genres that are now the focus of our teaching when they shared focus before? And how do other content-area teachers become enthused and educated about sharing the responsibility of teaching writing when it wasn't even on their radar before?

The chapters in this books are meant to be a soothing balm for all of those panicked about this educational tsunami coming our way. In fact, after sifting through some of these strategies, I am hopeful that you will also be encouraged about the Common Core world to come. For I see Common Core as an encouraging step in the right direction, a direction of more meaningful lessons and a focus on skills students will need for their future.

Will it be bumpy? Absolutely. Are we totally ready for the change? Of course not. Who is ever ready to throw their deck of cards up in the air? But it's a change that has to be, and if the classroom teacher is proactive in how they prepare for those changes, they can be a voice in deciding the powerful path for their state, their district, and their school site.

At the time I write this book, there are many possible scenarios still up in the air about the Common Core Standards and Assessments. However, what isn't unsure is the importance of writing in this Brave New Common Core World, and as a writing teacher, I realize that there are many teachers out there who will have to make far more changes than I do in order to achieve the goals before them. Better we should help each other make those changes by sharing what works in our classrooms. Together, we can examine the importance of writing in a Common Core world and in the real world. Together, we can help each other, teachers of all disciplines, adjust our practice in a way that excites us all to teach writing.

Change and upheaval are opportunities. Opportunities for teachers to design what they know is good, what they know will connect with students, and what they know will prepare those students for their futures. We may not clearly see the path that we will be taking, but if you have your toe in the pool of knowledge and are open to the change, you will be ahead of the train, laying down the tracks towards a better educational future for our students.

What's in a Name?

Every staff meeting, in every school, is the same. OK, so maybe that's hyperbolic, but I'm sure we've all been there at one time or another: an administrator comes in and declares the new instructional practice *du jour*. There are moans, probably heckles, and not a few eye rolls. "We've done this all before, haven't we?" teachers ask. After all, the educational pendulum swings often, and throughout a teacher's career, we see many supposedly silver bullets come and go. The Common Core movement, however, is no fad, and there are key differences between this era and those that came before it.

The fear, however, is that somehow writing for a Common Core movement will somehow stifle creativity and uniqueness. To me, that description sounds much more like the standardized movement of yore rather than this new era in education.

See, I see Common Core as recognizing creative thinking, creative writing, and creative ways of expressing oneself. It's about blended genres rather than categorized genres. It's about using technology to communicate, not struggling to teach technology in lieu of content. It's about the genre of real-world role-play rather than the genre of test taking.

I think if anything, the writers of the Common Core Standards fell short on branding. I mean, as much as I hated No Child Left Behind, nobody doubts the effectiveness of the name. How could anyone *not* pass NCLB? If you did, you'd clearly *want* to leave children behind, right?

But those who named the Common Core Standards did not come from the same school of marketing. They chose the word "common" because it meant that we all have goals in common. It meant we all share the burden of teaching some core skills and subjects.

But they neglected the other meaning of the word, the one that means bland and indistinct.

This relates to the outcry that went out as a result of a speech that went viral during the spring of 2012, the one where faculty member David McCullough Jr. from Wellesley High School claimed none of the students were special. (In fact, they were all, dare I say, "common"?) Parents were in an uproar.

So too are many teachers who struggled through the philosophies of the standardization movement when faced with this new "common" movement. These terms are ones that everyone is frightened have begun to define the American educational system. But I beg you to look beyond the terminology and start thinking of ways that the Common Core Standards are actually uncommon.

Going back to McCullough's speech. If you stick with it, you'll hear that the point really isn't that all students are common, but rather that being special is about how you contribute to society. That's what defines you. Common Core writing, I believe, relates to this goal because it asks students to think about what their brains contribute to a topic, not just the regurgitation of that topic.

Now, I'm not saying that the standards themselves are innovative. Nope. We've seen them in some way, shape, or form before. But what we haven't seen is the insistence to involve the 4Cs into our teaching. The 4Cs, first brought into our lexicon by the Partnership of 21st Century Skills, are noted as being:

- Critical thinking
- Collaboration
- Creativity
- Communication.

The Common Core Standards also include the promise to assess students based on those skills rather than asking teachers to just fit them in between the cracks in the time we have available after teaching our content. Thankfully, with assessment comes the requirement that we teach using those skills. The assessment tail that is wagging the dog is a much more interesting and valuable tail. *That's* what's new.

It's a tail that will test our students using online measures. It's a tail that will ask students to collaborate, brainstorm, and develop independently discovered questions to answer. It's a tail that will ask students to show their comprehension through writing.

However, the expectations of the Common Core Standards are more than just "Writing Across the Curriculum." These new goals ask that other disciplines don the hat of a writing teacher, not just use writing as a tool to deliver their content.

Unfortunately, teaching a particular subject is like working a muscle. If you have a single subject credential and you've been teaching math or science or history or an elective for the last ten years, you might need a little pumping up before teaching writing again for the first time.

The purpose of this book is twofold:

1. To help teachers who don't teach writing learn how to assign and assess writing comfortably and in a way that doesn't interfere with the content they also need to teach.
2. To help English/language arts teachers find unconventional ways to address the intense writing standards the Common Core Standards set upon us.

The key to both goals is, of course, collaboration. By working together in a tighter way than ever before, we can all support student achievement.

We need to look at the Common Core goals not so much as "I scratch your back, you scratch mine," but as a path we must travel together. We aren't doing each other a favor by incorporating these standards; we're achieving these new requirements in the only way we can . . . together and as a team.

The Importance of Transfer

Working together isn't only about helping each other do our jobs, it's also about developing a consistent web of expectations that envelopes students regardless of the room in which they are learning. And this consistent message of expectation helps support the transfer of information from classroom to classroom.

Our job as educators, and the goal of the Common Core Standards, is to prepare students for the world beyond school. Yet this can't happen without some consistency between the classrooms. There are a few skills, strategies, and philosophies that can be shared between the classrooms. The use of writing is one of them.

The way I see it, there are two levels of transference that a student must be able to accomplish. They must be able, on a grand scale, to transfer what they learn in

K12 education to the world outside of school. They must also, within our walls, be able to transfer what they learn from class to class.

Sure we all hope that students remember their multiplication tables when they walk into history class or facts about Thomas Jefferson when they enter a Spanish class. But when I talk about transference, I'm talking more about skills than content. A student being able to recall facts is not as important as, say, being able to discover facts themselves. A student being able to regurgitate information in isolation is not as important as being able to collaborate with peers no matter the room in which their feet take them.

According to Linda Darling-Hammond, Stanford University professor and leader in educational policy reform, the 4Cs were de-emphasized during the standardized movement in the past. As a result, transference and application suffered. She acknowledges that, "the skill that may be the trickiest to teach and test . . . is the student's ability to transfer and apply existing knowledge to a problem in a new context." To solve this, the goal of the Common Core Standards is in making subjects more applicable so that transference is more organic. She says, "in mathematics, for example, we wouldn't necessarily just give kids these problem sets but engage them in identifying, framing, and solving real-world problems that would use those problem sets."

That's where the Partnership's 4Cs come in. They serve as a shortlist of skills that we need to insist on no matter where the students roam.

In every classroom, a student must be expected to collaborate. That student must be asked to work with others, come to consensus, move on, contribute, share the air, and pull their own weight.

In every classroom, a student must be expected to use critical thinking. If a student can't recall every fact he or she learned in other classrooms, that's fine. However, that student needs to be able to use Internet literacy and problem-solving to find their own answers. They need to be able to unearth problems independently and pose solutions.

In every classroom, a student must be expected to use creativity. They must be asked to create solutions, create ways to display their knowledge, and create ways to get their content across.

In every classroom, a student must be expected to communicate. And that's where writing comes in. No matter your subject, you can't escape it.

And that's the key to transferring and applying knowledge outside of any classroom. A student must encounter these skills in every classroom so that they can't escape developing their 4Cs muscle.

Imagine if, when you were learning how to drive, you could only drive around your block. You would never learn to drive on any other kind of road or highway. Imagine if you were at culinary school and you only cooked in one kitchen using the same supplies over and over. You would never know how to handle the equipment or the environment of a restaurant that may want to hire you.

So is it with our classrooms. If we expect knowledge to transfer, we can't teach in isolation. The skills we identify as those that are the most important cannot remain locked inside one content-area classroom.

And for the first time, we don't need to work to identify those skills, and we don't need to fight to justify their importance. The standards and the assessments designed for the Common Core give us that list of skills by peppering the 4Cs throughout the language of the sample tests, and because they are formally assessed, there should be no debate that one must use these strategies to teach regardless of the subject taught.

However, this new collaborative curricular movement is still thought of as relatively new and intimidating by many secondary teachers. After all, many of us design, teach, and assess in isolation. Yet I believe this to be an antiquated methodology.

Only consistency will aid in information and skill transference. Only if we all adopt certain key targets, like particular real-life standards in how students must communicate their knowledge, will school life apply more to real life.

A Little Educational History to Get the Ball Rolling

In 2010 I was in a professional slump. I had begun to see some patterns in my teaching that I was bored with, and I knew that if I was bored, so were my students. I began to use test prep as the compass for my lessons, and when asked the inevitable question of "Why do we have to learn this?" I caught myself almost responding, "Because it's on the test."

I looked at myself and saw that the path I was headed towards was one that I would not enjoy walking down for another two decades. And if I didn't enjoy teaching, I knew my students would not enjoy learning.

So I got down on one knee (metaphorically, of course) and I renewed my vows to my profession.

Since then, I have dedicated my classroom practice to project-based learning. My assessments became meshed in real-life scenarios. My lessons asked students to use skills meant for their future-selves. My theory was, "if it didn't appear in real life, then it was not going to appear in my classroom." It was a vow that has helped guide my teaching ever since.

True, the main reason I remarried teaching was because I was feeling the pull of the undertow of stagnation. But another reason I rededicated myself to a different kind of meaningful instruction was because my knowledge of educational assessment history (and its subsequent stagnation) grew. And with my knowledge came a renewed vigor to fight against antiquated methodology.

Here's what I learned and how I came to my own personal and professional eureka moment:

Timeline of History of Assessments (and Some Other Pertinent Educational Information)

1914—First multiple-choice standardized test invented to address the influx of students into the school system and to assess "lower-order thinking" among the masses

1930s—First Scantron invented

1953—Differentiation pops up as a concept in an Educational Leadership article by Carleton W. Washburne called "Adjusting the Program to the Child"

1980s–1990s—State standards are instated

2006—~7 percent of all students in public schools are labeled as gifted

2010—~11 percent of students are labeled special ed in public schools

2012—~ 11 percent = # of English language learners in public school classrooms

When I looked really clearly at these facts, it was undeniable that we were assessing the same way we have been since 1914, but our population and knowledge and culture were vastly different. Now, clearly when one thinks about all those kids who are being tested on the same information, in the same methods (bubbling with a pencil), one can clearly see the need for a massive overhaul.

I looked at data, and I looked in the mirror. I realized that I had my own accountability as a participant in a mediocre system. And I thought long and hard about the damage that standardization was doing to innovation in this country and to both my students' deeper knowledge and my own enthusiasm for teaching. As a result, I signed my own mental contract promising to make my classroom richer than it ever was.

And then along came the Common Core Standards, and I realized that despite all of their problems and perhaps premature implementation, they glowed with potential. For that's what I find so hopeful about them: they are intended to bring authenticity and real-world scenarios to assessments. And in education, as we all know, assessments wag the lesson-planning dog.

Here are the pluses in the upcoming assessments as I see them:

- The multiple-choice tests are computerized. I hear a lot of concern about the training the kids will need to take these tests, but I, frankly, am thrilled. I mean, kids are bound to click more accurately than they bubble with their #2 pencils!

- The multiple-choice tests for some of the tests are intended to be adaptive. The questions will adjust to the levels of the students who answer them.

- There will be a performance-based element to the assessments that will allow a student to showcase their knowledge in a method other then clicking a multiple-choice response.

- Students will be asked to upload projects that will require a variety of skills to complete: collaboration, writing, reading, technology integration, etc.

- There will be a greater expectation in every classroom that students will use writing as a means to communicate all disciplinary content.

Therefore, it seems that even while the conversation still focuses on STEM subjects (see President Obama's 2012 DNC speech calling for stronger STEM teachers and learners as an educational goal for this country), it is also shifting to envelop universal writing as a means to communicate any content. After all, a mathematician who can't write is not one that can be a leader on a global scale, just as a scientist who cannot write cannot prove or improve the innovations to come.

The pendulum of curriculum is swinging not to exclude, but to include. And while it sounds like we are once again forced to "do it all," the fact is that the Common Core is instead asking us to "do what matters." For we know, based on research such as Judith Langer's and Arthur Applebee's 2010 study on the subject, that when we exclude communication in our attempt to concentrate on content, we see an immediate decrease in writing ability in our students. That's bad for the schools, bad for our students' futures, and bad for this country. In fact, in a recent article in *The Atlantic*, Applebee cited current assessments as one of the reasons student writing quality is not ideal. He said,

> The high-stakes tests that drive curricula in most states require very little writing, and that in turn has driven writing out of many classrooms. The National Assessment of Educational Progress reported earlier this month that in 2011, 40 to 41 percent of public school students at grades 8 and 12 were given less than a page of writing homework in a typical week. In fact some 14 percent of twelfth graders reported being asked to do *no* writing for homework at all.

In the view of Linda Friedrich, the Director of Research and Evaluation for the National Writing Project (NWP),

> the Common Core's emphasis on writing instruction and the role of writing in other disciplines is already beginning to shift schools' focus toward writing . . . The inclusion of writing and research tasks in the new assessments being developed by PARCC and Smarter Balanced also provides a policy press towards teaching writing.

I believe this focus on writing is not a step back in education, but rather a step forward.

Now, look, I'm not a Pollyanna. I know there are schools that might not have the money for the technology or they might not have the funds for the professional development to train teachers. They might not have support from administrators who acknowledge the absolute necessity to collaborate but who can't come through with the time. I know that there are test design companies making money hand over fist with this new wave of assessments.

However, rather than focus on the smog that can be educational policy and marketing, I choose instead to focus on aspects of the Common Core movement that aren't about the politics, aren't about the publishing companies, and aren't about what's lacking. Instead, I choose to focus on how these new expectations might very well result in a better education for our students. When I think about the pluses, I find within myself more enthusiasm in this evolution than dread.

For my last book, I crowd-sourced a number of teachers to find out the list of college and career ready skills that they felt were the most important and valuable to teach. The list was inspired by the work from the 4Cs' creators, the Partnership for 21st Century Skills. P21 is an organization comprised of both business leaders and folks in higher education. The original list of skills that I analyzed as the most important skills for students leaving K12 were as follows:

- Collaboration
- Communication
- Problem-solving
- Decision-making
- Understanding bias
- Leadership
- Questioning
- Independent learning
- Compromise
- Summarizing
- Sharing the air
- Persuasion
- Goal-setting.

The classroom teachers then took that list and honed it to five skills that they felt students most needed. Their essential list of skills were as follows:

- Collaboration
- Communication
- Problem-solving
- Questioning
- Independent learning.

The way I see the Common Core Standards, the lens through which I look when determining my next pathway through lesson planning, design, and assessments, is that these new standards are addressing these same skills in a way that past assessments did not. Perhaps we are on the right path towards more accurate assessments of our country's students.

The strategies in this book are about what you can do in your classroom right now to help prepare students to use those college and career ready skills. It doesn't matter if you are an English teacher, a math teacher, a science teacher, a history teacher, an electives teacher, or a PE teacher, these are techniques, strategies, and structures that you can start using now so that you can say you are involved in this possible wave of best practices in education.

Will there be pushback? Of course. There always is when there is a new movement upon us. But if it does turn out to be a better, more innovative, and engaging way to teach and learn, who wants to say that they were on the side that pushed back against such possibility?

In these pages, we will focus on what great, forward-thinking, Common Core focused teachers are already doing and what each department can do to contribute to the education of their clients: the students. For we are no longer teaching behind closed doors. We are meant to be a collaborative group of adults working together, using a combination of common strategies and strategies uniquely tuned to our own styles.

What once was this:

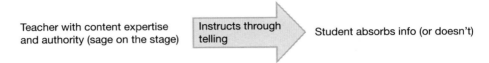

Teacher with content expertise and authority (sage on the stage) | Instructs through telling | Student absorbs info (or doesn't)

FIGURE I.1

should now be this:

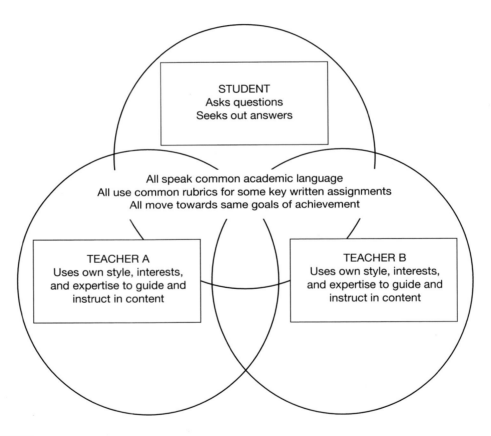

STUDENT
Asks questions
Seeks out answers

All speak common academic language
All use common rubrics for some key written assignments
All move towards same goals of achievement

TEACHER A
Uses own style, interests, and expertise to guide and instruct in content

TEACHER B
Uses own style, interests, and expertise to guide and instruct in content

FIGURE I.2

Or, as my eighth grade student Grant doodled:

What was once this:

FIGURE I.3

is so much better as this:

FIGURE I.4

Every teacher brings something wonderful to our school sites, but we must be encouraged to work more closely together as well, regardless of our disciplines. This book is meant to aid in creating the common language and common structure of communicating our individual contents that unite us all as a school site and as a profession.

So open up your doors, flip on your computers, "follow" each other, and let's collaborate on some common writing strategies for this Common Core world.

Writing as the Universal Subject

The ability to write well is a universal goal. It is vastly important in the success of a student and in the success of an adult. Think back on how you got your job. It required writing: a persuasive or informational cover letter, a resume, recommendations, perhaps a mission statement. Perhaps you even put together a multi-genre project of sorts in the form of a portfolio. Think about the people you encounter every day outside of school: grocery clerk, mailman, colleague, administrator, AT&T gal on the phone, lawyer, doctor, receptionist for that doctor, etc. Each of them used writing to get to where they are, currently use writing to communicate with people in their daily lives, and will use writing to get to where they need to be.

But to really get down to the nitty-gritty of just how vital writing is in our everyday lives, sometimes a visual is the way to go. Therefore, I want you to keep a log. Don't worry. It doesn't have to be a concrete-you-must-write-and-you-will-be-tested-after-you-finish-this-book kind of log. No, it can be a mental log if you prefer. The log is to give you a real accounting of the writing that you do every day. After all, when you are figuring out where your money goes each month, you write every penny down to honestly assess its disappearance. Today, I'm going to ask you to think in a similarly Type A way. I want you to spend a week identifying just how much you write and the genre of writing you are doing. For instance, are you writing an email to explain to your principal why you can't do your afternoon supervision? I bet there are elements of narrative in there. Are you commenting on someone's Facebook post by posting your own link for further sharing of resources? This might be informational. Are you leaving a note for your spouse to please pick up the dry cleaning? Definitely persuasive.

In other words, I want you to create a mental log that records the following:

1. Date

2. Time

3. Task—what was the purpose of your writing?

4. Genre—what style of writing did you use?

5. Number of revisions—How many revisions did you make to each entry before you called it a final draft or ready to be sent or seen by its audience? Did you catch a spelling error before pressing "send"? Did you decide to reword a sentence to ensure that your colleagues understood your intent?

Play along and fill out the ledger in Table I.1 mentally or physically. Track how much writing you do in a week, even just a day. Include every word, every emoticon :), every penny.

I had you do this little exercise to really bring home the fact that writing is a universal skill that every human in this country, and that includes students, must do well. However, to accomplish this, a student can't be only using writing, and getting feedback on writing, forty-five minutes a day for five days a week. Nope. It's too darn vast a task. Therefore, it can't only fall to language arts to request, assign, and assess.

That is where you come in. No matter what your subject matter, you have a role to play here in teaching writing in a Common Core world. But nobody expects you to be able to do it without training and professional development (see Chapter 9 for more on professional development).

However, you don't have to halt all the great stuff and exciting content you teach. No way; no how. Teaching writing is about inserting your own content and guiding students to communicate that content to the best of their ability. Learning to write takes forming a ring of adults around each student, a ring made up of all their teachers (and hopefully their parents too, but don't hold your breath), that all support the same goal.

Before we begin, however, I want to make sure we're all speaking the same language and looking at the same figures.

TABLE I.1 Writing Ledger

Date	Time	Task	Genre	Number of Revisions (if any)
6/10/12	2:16pm	Email to department	Informational	3

According to the Common Core Standards, under their subheading, "Shared responsibility for students' literacy development," the document provides data on both reading and writing expectations. Table I.2 outlines clearly the percentages that students should be encountering and interacting with certain genres of text throughout their time in school.

Just a brief note here: The Common Core Standards refer to literary writing (narrative) as "conveying experience." The goal here is to focus more on creative non-fiction or on literary fiction that utilizes various literary elements. Once learned, the overall focus for these literary devices downsizes as a genre all its own and instead is meant to be folded into other kinds of writing. Thus, the multi-genre or blended genre essay incorporates various writing elements by grade 12. This does not mean that narrative disappears altogether (see Chapter 4 for more on teaching narrative strategies that align with the Common Core). It means that skills and techniques used in narrative writing should be interwoven into other writings as well.

If you do the math, you'll see that to reach these goals takes working together. There is no way that ELA can achieve them alone. And, in return, ELA has a role in using more science and history and other informational, rigorous texts in their literacy program. More on that later.

So let's break it down for an average, Common Core infused eighth grader: (infodoodle in Figure I.5 courtesy of my student, Grant):

Average school day = 6 hours (360 minutes/day)

35 percent of a school day should be spent doing informational writing

Forty-five minutes/day of middle school ELA time = 12.5 percent

35 percent minus 12.5 percent = 22 percent shortfall.

To do all this takes input from every teacher. In fact, the standards say that while there are two sections of 6–12 standards, one for ELA and the other for the different disciplines, that is because the "division reflects the unique, time-honored place of ELA teachers in developing students' literacy skills while at the same time recognizing that teachers in other areas must play a role in this development as well."

However, the way that middle schools and high schools are set up, each teacher in his or her own little corner, flies in the face of curriculum integration. So it's up to us to open our doors and ensure that we share certain common goals.

TABLE I.2 Breakdown of Writing According to the Common Core

Grade Level	Literary (To Convey Experience)—Writing	Information—Writing	Argument—Writing
4	35%	35%	30%
8	30%	35%	30%
12	20%	40%	40%

FIGURE I.5

William Zinsser writes in his book, *Writing to Learn*, that

> contrary to popular belief, writing isn't something that only "writers" do; writing is a basic skill for getting through life . . . [it] isn't a special language that belongs to English teachers and a few other sensitive souls who have a "gift for words." Writing is thinking on paper. Anyone who thinks clearly should be able to write clearly—about any subject at all.

Now, while I'm hoping that my little quantitative reasoning is rationale enough, the next place to look for evidence of the need for interdisciplinary writing is in the language of the standards themselves.

Here's how it breaks down as a word cloud (Figure I.6). You'll notice that repeating words are bigger than words that appear less frequently. To construct this word cloud that I made using Wordle, I inputted standards from both math and language arts. It is a visual way to see that there are clear overlaps in what we need to all be teaching.

If you haven't looked at a word cloud such as this before, the point is to insert text and visually see the most important concepts pop up as the larger text. In this case, I entered the information from the Common Core Standards on both the ELA College and Career Readiness in Writing as well as the Standards for Mathematical Practice. As you can see, there are some real outstanding points that

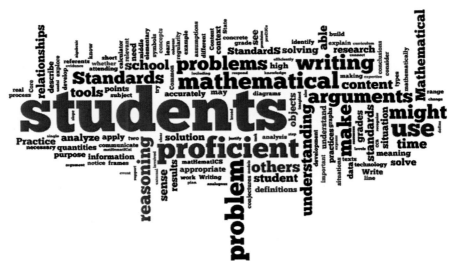

FIGURE I.6

make the argument for teaching writing across the curriculum. The biggest words that stress the importance of a universal writing curriculum are as follows:

- Understanding
- Problem
- Reasoning
- Writing
- Analyze
- Make
- Simulation
- Meaning
- Describe
- Argument
- Purpose.

Of course, the biggest word here is the most important of them all: Students. After all, it is the mission of our schools to educate the students in the skills that will prepare them for their futures. And with the new Common Core Standards, and the expectations for all of the subjects that go hand in hand with them, we will hopefully educate them better than ever.

Yet many teachers in different disciplines still wonder why. Why do they need to focus on writing at all as a means to communicate their content? That is because of the real-world application that writing holds. It is unavoidable. Writing is asked of people in every career, in every college course, and on every path. However, to teach writing doesn't mean detracting from glorious content; instead look at it this way: writing helps exploit one's content in a more applicable way.

But don't just take it from me. Check out these following resources at your leisure. The first explores the less structured expectation of writing as it relates to higher education. The others are each from scientists who share their need to write and how it relates to their scientific studies:

NWP Radio: What is College Writing Today?
http://www.nwp.org/cs/public/print/resource/3934
Why I Write Essays:
http://www.nwp.org/cs/public/print/resource/3731
http://www.nwp.org/cs/public/print/resource/3702
http://www.nwp.org/cs/public/print/resource/3701

Therefore, it goes without saying that every teacher must carry the burden of responsibility in teaching these areas of writing. And when I say teaching, I don't just mean assigning an essay or short-answer response and then scoring it on its content alone. I mean donning the costume of the writing teacher and being responsible for passing on the guidance as the best writer in the room. Assess them on content, but also on their ability to communicate that content. This doesn't always occur to teachers who don't teach writing per se. Perhaps they see themselves as the best scientist in the room or the best historian in the room, but writer? Not necessarily.

Well, it's time we change that perception of ourselves. We can no longer be defined by our content. We cannot be "math teachers" or "ELA teachers." Instead, we are all "educators." And as educators, we need to be united by some universally adopted best practices if we are to be universally effective.

The best practices of . . .

■ Integrating interdisciplinary content across the curriculum
■ Using a common academic language
■ Using project-based learning to assess and help drive instruction
■ Teaching students to develop high-level questions to indicate comprehension
■ Recognizing learning in informal as well as formal assessments
■ Bringing in real-world scenarios in our teaching and learning
■ Having students produce multi-genre projects that are scored on writing quality as well as content
■ Modeling writing

Educator and author Kelly Gallagher stresses this last point, that the teacher is the "best writer in the room" who must show students "how to grapple with this mysterious thing we call writing." Just as a math teacher shows students how to solve a problem and narrates their thinking process, so must that same math teacher model the quantitative writing a student will have to use in order to support their answer. (See Chapter 7 for more strategies on this topic.)

But who can blame a science and elective and math teacher who are experts in their own content area but who are not writers themselves? The chapters ahead are meant to help create a few threads of alignment between classes so that a student understands what's expected in each room he or she enters. All teachers, therefore, hold students to the writing standards agreed upon by all of the departments in a school. These chapters are intended to give all teachers strategies to teach writing to support both their content and the Common Core movement upon us.

A Brief Note on the Need for Tweens and Teens to Write

Once a student enters middle school, their world becomes more segregated. What was once a day filled with fewer teachers, more blended learning, more interactivity, and more outlets to express himself or herself, quickly changes.

The typical secondary student's day is statistically filled with more lectures, fewer kinesthetic opportunities, fewer minutes of interacting with other peers, and less time devoted to expressing oneself. Yet this last limitation comes at the exact time when they need expressive outlets the most.

Their brains are wired to give opinions, to form judgments, and to analyze the world around them. Writing helps them to express and analyze by giving them an authentic outlet. Steve Peha of "Teaching That Makes Sense" says it best when he writes:

> There's nothing more frustrating than being a teenager . . . But often it's not what students are going through that's so hard, it's their inability to make sense of it. I notice a dramatic difference in the attitudes and behaviors of teenagers who write well versus those who don't. Being unable to express oneself is one of the most frustrating feelings a human being can experience. And it is often this frustration that lies at the heart of what drives teenagers to be so rebellious, so depressed, and so difficult to inspire.

Giving teenagers the outlet to express themselves through writing will not only help them socially–emotionally, but will also help them interact with your content, whatever that content might be.

I liken elementary school to a beach with the kids all learning how to advance towards the water. But they have a lot of choices. They can build sandcastles, play volleyball, and eat sandwiches on a towel. High school is like the open ocean. It's vast, so it can be scary, but they've learned to swim and are now deciding whether they want to scuba dive or swim on the surface. Middle school, however, is the tidal shore. The water crashes over them; it tumbles them around, and they can't yell without water filling their lungs. Their direction seems out of their control just when they want to control it the most.

It's when students hit middle school that they need lessons in how to call for help. They need lessons in how to find the bottom and push off. They need lessons in how to express their fear, and ideas in how to become buoyant. By high school, those students must learn to do more than doggie-paddle. They must show an endurance in the water in order to reach another shore.

Writing is a pool in which they can learn to swim. Regardless of your subject matter, you are their coach as they paddle with words, stroke using sentences, and dive through paragraphing.

CHAPTER

1

The Common Core Standards as a Meaningful Guide, Not an Instruction Manual

> The common core state standards are a set of learning skills that all American students should achieve, not a federal curriculum. They set the benchmarks and guidelines for what each student should learn, not how or what teachers teach.
>
> ("A Parent's Guide to the Common Core Standards")

As I've said before, assessments tend to drive instruction. However, as we know, that isn't the best way to teach. In fact, it turns out, it's not a particularly good way to assess either.

In the introduction of this book, I listed a few things I like about the Common Core Standards and the assessments to come. I like that the multiple-choice tests are computerized. I like that some of them may be adaptive because then they are more tailored to the individual. I applaud the fact that they include a requirement that is more than just a multiple-choice component in that they are also asking for a performance-based element that reflects the use of skills other than simple information download.

In other words, I believe that while test taking is still its own genre, the powers that be are moving towards a more real-world aligned practice. What is being asked is closer to what students will have to do when they are no longer in our school systems.

So, for that reason, I don't believe that there is one method or philosophy to achieve these standards. Perhaps this next era will give teachers more flexibility to select the methods they feel would best accomplish the goal. Let's hope so.

However, regardless of what the Common Core (CC) assessments may ask of us, the fact is that we should have more flexibility in our own classroom assessments. It is our responsibility as teachers to ensure that our classroom or district assessments are meaningful. We can't wait for state or federal tests to do it for us. It may never happen. Therefore, I'm going to go so far as to say: ditch test stress and don't worry about it.

Don't panic. I'm not saying, "don't care." I'm saying do the job you know you should do, and I believe that scores will fall into place. Use the Common Core

Standards as a guide to what needs to be taught, but use your talents, your experience, and your common sense to get the students there.

Having said that, I wanted to just brush off a couple of old tried and true educative philosophies that relate to writing across the content areas. By doing so, I'm hoping to remind readers of the powerful learning that can happen when engagement is combined with simplicity.

In terms of student engagement, there is nothing more powerful than Project-Based Learning, and for the purposes of this book, project-based writing. In terms of simplicity, especially for those who are unfamiliar with assigning and assessing writing in the classroom, you can't get more straightforward than using the 6 Traits as a guide for writing quality. These two practices can be used regardless of the content and regardless of the educational movement we are facing. In other words, no matter whether we are facing having to hit a list of specific state standards, national standards, Common Core Standards, 22nd century global standards, or mythical intergalactic standards, good teaching practices work.

Therefore, if we think of the Common Core Standards as a guide, not a manual, it is vital to know that you don't need to ditch what you know works. In this chapter, I want to remind you of (or perhaps even introduce you to) a few practices that really work.

Therefore, in the spirit of honoring both the old with the new, let's first do a little review of Project-Based Learning and the 6 Traits.

Welcoming Back an Old Friend: Project-Based Learning (or, in this case, Project-Based Writing)

Recently, I had an awakening of sorts in my own practice: *I am NOT going to teach so test-driven,* I told myself. *I'm tired of the five-paragraph essay! Where does it exist anywhere but in school?* Instead, I decided that everything I did from here on in would have some connection to the world outside of school. The plan: to immerse my lessons and my classroom assessments in authenticity. And test scores be darned.

OK, so maybe I wasn't *that* confident. Nevertheless, I went ahead with my plans and devised units based on project-based writing. I want to take a moment to review this concept with readers because I think that, while it is old news to many, we tend to lose perspective about the basic principles of PBL when we are faced with what we believe to be a strict checklist, an instruction manual, of standards. We look at the checklist and start to organize our practice around test prep rather than around real-world application. However, I think if one were to reexamine PBL through the lens of Common Core, you'll see that you don't need to sacrifice quality teaching practices to achieve these newer standards.

Now, I'm lucky. I work in a district and, more specifically, in a school, that permits me to develop units and lessons that align to our tests. They also allow me my better judgment in how to prepare for them so that I am not lock step with other teachers. We are all allowed our own style, and thus appeal to a wider variety of learners.

I have to also give credit where credit is due: the past era of economic depression and budget cuts actually had a lot to do with the freedom I was permitted as a creative teacher; with no textbook adoptions in sight and antiquated textbooks falling apart on our shelves, this also became an era of opportunity for teacher-supported supplementation of the curriculum. As a result, I have been able to choose authentic lessons and authentic classroom assessments. At the start of this more meaningful educative journey, I hoped that our more traditional district assessments scores would reflect that deeper learning. In the end, I was right.

However, my luck is not the norm. Too many teachers are told that the classroom tests, the district tests, the state tests, and the federal tests are the driving force of the curriculum. They are not permitted the freedom to use their own training, their own expertise, and their own instinct to look beyond the test prep lessons.

Additionally, not all teachers are eager to start trusting themselves to develop materials. So many have been brainwashed. Yep, I said it. Brainwashed. I think some teachers have actually started to believe what the media, politicos, and textbook companies would have us think: that we aren't capable of creating. That all we can do to prepare for standardized tests is regurgitate the canned lessons from the textbook and test prep companies. But I believe that once teachers rediscover some of the benefits of project-based learning, and more specifically for the purposes of this book, project-based writing, it's hard to go back to a canned program. See, one size does not fit all when it comes to engaging students.

If our country wants to cultivate innovative students, it needs to allow for innovation in our classroom. Innovation in our students begins with innovative teachers; and innovative teachers cannot thrive in a standardized environment.

Project-based learning allows for innovation. For those who perhaps have heard the term but who aren't fully clear what it means in the classroom, it is a way of teaching that is more guidance than authority. In project-based learning, students jump into learning content by engaging in rigorous projects as an end result to their efforts. Many practitioners of project-based learning also use problem-based learning wherein the students discover issues or problems that need to be solved and learning happens throughout the process of solving the issue.

Now, while I know it's not kosher to use the terms interchangeably, I do believe, however, that they are related, and I teach now using both: problems designated by students for solution and projects designed to communicate the best way in which to solve them. Writing is always interwoven throughout both the lessons and the assessments. After all, a student must be able to use writing to communicate his or her findings or solutions.

In other words, rather than the daily use of worksheets or the routine of daily whole classroom instruction, the teacher hands over the badge of being the only content-area expert, and allows students to build up their own knowledge with more authentic goals to reach in order to prove their learning.

Project-based learning is how teachers who cannot control the content they teach can at least control the way in which they teach it. PBL stresses communication over content.

And it's vital for middle and secondary students. In fact, the New York Department of Education's white paper, "Project Based Learning: Inspiring Middle School Students to Engage in Deep and Active Learning," states that,

> The middle school years are challenging. We struggle with keeping students academically engaged during these years of tremendous change. Because projects build on authentic learning tasks that engage and motivate students, middle school is an ideal time to integrate project-based learning. Projects encourage students to encounter, and struggle with, important and "big" ideas. Project-based learning in all content areas (e.g., language arts, social studies, math, science, visual and performing arts, health) shifts the focus of teaching and learning from a set of known facts to a process modeled on the ways that experts in the field think and work.

Project-based learning is about role-play. It is about authenticity. And it is about application. Good teaching, meaningful teaching, project-based teaching, therefore, hits the new standards.

For example, the new expectation of collaboration appears in the Speaking and Listening section of the standards:

Speaking and Listening: flexible communication and collaboration

Including but not limited to skills necessary for formal presentations, the Speaking and Listening standards require students to develop a range of broadly useful oral communication and interpersonal skills. Students must learn to work together, express and listen carefully to ideas, integrate information from oral, visual, quantitative, and media sources, evaluate what they hear, use media and visual displays strategically to help achieve communicative purposes, and adapt speech to context and task.

Beginning in kindergarten, students must:

■   With guidance and support from adults, explore a variety of digital tools to produce and publish writing, including in collaboration with peers.

And as a college and career ready skill, students must:

■   Comprehension and Collaboration: Prepare for and participate effectively in a range of conversations and collaborations with diverse partners, building on others' ideas and expressing their own clearly and persuasively.

Students must also:

■   Engage effectively in a range of collaborative discussions (one-on-one, in groups, and teacher-led) with diverse partners on grade [level] topics and texts, building on others' ideas and expressing their own clearly.

- Follow agreed–upon rules for discussions (e.g., gaining the floor in respectful ways, listening to others with care, speaking one at a time about the topics and texts under discussion).

- Ask questions to check understanding of information presented, stay on topic, and link their comments to the remarks of others.

So once I realized that PBL aligned directly to the assessments to come, and that writing was now a universal expectation in all content areas, I spun the concept for a writing focus and rededicated my instructional practice towards project–based writing. That is, my content-area writing units became based in real-world scenarios for real-world audiences using writing as the means to communicate the answer to real-world problems.

One unit in particular was called the DARPA/NASA unit (an informational and persuasive writing project which you can read more about in Chapter 6). It focused on a real conference that was happening in Florida where scientists, futurists, and science-fiction writers were all called together to brainstorm how humans can colonize a planet within a hundred years. My students used the conference proposal template to form their own hypotheses, pitching their findings using the format of executive summary (see Chapter 5 for more information on summary writing). In the end, someone at CalState got wind of our project, and my classes in California were invited to present at the actual gathering in Florida via video-conferencing software.

Another project-based writing unit focused on a blend of advocacy and memoir similar to those performed for TED conferences (see Chapter 3 for more on this unit). In the end, each student performed their TED-esque speech for their own class period, and then evaluated each other to select the best presentations to perform in front of a wider audience as a book drive for our school library.

And so my year progressed with project-based writing as my focus. All of the units, however, had commonalities. They allowed students to:

- Choose their own topics,

- Create the rubrics upon which they evaluated their peers and themselves,

- Produce final drafts that used blended genres (informational, argument, narrative) rather than merely a single-genre essay (see Chapter 6 for more on multi-genre projects),

- Include a multi-modal presentation (like a website or an oral presentation) that wove together text, visuals, music, and video.

In the end, the students learned more than they ever did before. And when asked on a test to use the standard five-paragraph format, they were able to transfer their knowledge of good writing to the more rigid structure of testing. And my scores? Well, I found that the students who participated in the project-based learning units performed better on the district assessments than any of my classes in the past that had not.

I have little doubt that it was my leap of faith into project-based writing that got them there. I also have little doubt that I will never look back.

I have shared some information on the units in my own language arts classroom, but you'll notice that the content the students researched was influenced by content outside of my own. The DARPA/NASA unit was rich in science. The TED unit was rich in many advocacy topics that ranged from environmental issues to political ones. However, I am not the content-area expert in any of these topics. I am, however, a guide in how to communicate those topics.

There is a place for project-based writing in any classroom of any discipline because real-world writing is a skill that can and should transfer from math to history, from PE to art, from ELA to science, from school to the outside world. That's what makes it meaningful.

There are many reasons to begin using (or fight for the right to continue using) project-based writing.

Ten Reasons to Teach Using Project-Based Writing

1. It is an organic way to integrate all Core subjects: math, science, history, and language arts.
2. It proves to students that imagination and creativity are connected to research and expository writing.
3. It hits all the major elements of the higher level of Bloom's Taxonomy: analysis, evaluation, and creation.
4. It allows students to choose their format of showing what they know. As a result, the buy-in for the quality of the final project is tremendous.
5. Students develop projects individualized, unique, and specific from each other.
6. It is a powerful way to incorporate all multiple intelligences: visual, audio, kinesthetic, musical, linguistic, logical, etc.
7. It desegregates non-fiction and fiction, blending the two.
8. It integrates the Core subjects with non-Core subjects, potentially using technology, art, music, etc.
9. It is a rigorous assessment requiring high levels of thought and communication.
10. It requires use of the entire writing process from brainstorm through revision, editing, and final draft regardless of the genres picked and the topic chosen.

Suffice it to say, all of this equates to preparing students for a Common Core world. Interested in other resources on learning about project-based learning, problem-based learning, or project-based writing? See the list of resources that follow:

- The George Lucas Educational Foundation's Edutopia website (check out their archive of PBL blogs posts, webinars, and free downloadable instructional guides)
- *Reinventing Project-Based Learning: Your Field Guide to Real-World Projects in the Digital Age*, ISTE Publications
- *Students Taking Charge: Inside the Learner-Active, Technology-Infused Classroom*, Eye on Education

- Project Based Learning Handbook: A Guide to Standards-Focused PBL for Middle and High School Teachers, Buck Institute for Education.

Brushing the Dust Off of the 6 Traits (+ 2)

I mentioned before that if students understood the basic elements of good writing, at their most simplistic foundational blocks, then they could write to any prompt for any purpose. In this next section, I break down the elements of good, meaningful writing so that any teacher can begin to incorporate writing as a foundational expectation for his or her students.

Many students do not see meaning in the work asked of them without a teacher spelling it out, and even then they might not believe it. Additionally, many students don't naturally see how school aligns to life, and as I discussed in the introduction, school hasn't done much up until recently to dissuade that reputation.

Using the 6 Traits helps to bridge the gap between school life and real life because it applies to every writing genre. Therefore, if we treat the Common Core Standards more as a guide and less as a manual, this frees up teachers to use more general practices to address them. The 6 Traits could be understood to be a more universal practice for the universal subject of writing.

It's our responsibility to help students realize that there is purpose to our lessons and that what we are learning is important, not just "because it's on the test." One of the ways to make writing more meaningful is to broaden our definition of what good writing accomplishes, and broaden our strategies in teaching writing. I think the 6 Traits does that very well by giving teachers a more universal way to teach, assign, and assess writing.

Ruth Culham, "The Trait Lady" who first coined the seventh trait as Presentation in the 6 Traits + 1 movement, says that this shortlist of writing characteristics "represents a language that empowers students and teachers to communicate about qualities of writing." The traits help to universally assess all kinds of writing and also help to define writing, a skill that can be subjective and ambiguous for both students and teachers. By defining a catchall list of guidelines for any teacher, of any subject, writing becomes more applicable and authentic for the students and the teaching of writing becomes more accessible to all teachers.

One of the things I like about the 6 Traits is that it's short and sweet. Shorter is better in terms of making rules that students must utilize in all classrooms. Less is more to students when it comes to transferring skills between classrooms or between school and beyond.

Having a cursory knowledge of this shortlist is valuable to any teacher of any discipline. Imagine the powerful writing that could come out of a school if every teacher, of every discipline, not only had these posted, but also understood a foundational knowledge of these traits enough to hold students accountable for the writing that they produce.

The 6 Traits (+ 2) as I describe them to my students are as follows:

1. **Voice**—Who is the audience that you are writing for? How does that help you make decisions about your writing voice? Is your voice unique to other voices out there?

2. **Organization**—What's the purpose of the writing, and how can you structure it to get your ideas across clearly for your reader?

3. **Ideas**—What is the content, the subject matter, the topic, that is under scrutiny? How are your thoughts original and/or do they bring an original spin to commonly understand information?

4. **Sentence fluency**—Do your sentences take your reader on a roller-coaster ride? Are they short and long? Do they use different conventions like commas, semi-colons, colons, etc., to bring texture to your writing? Do they flow together like a smooth riding coaster or are they rickety and jumpy like an old, wooden coaster?

5. **Conventions**—Is your spelling, grammar, and punctuation correct such that it doesn't interfere with your readers' understanding of your writing? Do your errors get in the way of the ideas you want to convey? Do they distract your reader from your point?

6. **Word choice**—Are you using the highest level and most appropriate words possible? Are they persuasive or informative or descriptive? Is your writing full of content-specific words, academic words, and juicy words that drip down your chin?

7. **Presentation**—In the end, have you packaged your writing in a way that lures people in to learn what you have to say? Besides just being neat, how have you chosen to present your writing to the public in a way that is tempting to read?

8. **Real-world application** (this one's my addition)—How does your writing relate to the world around you? How have you made your writing meaningful to others, either through the information/content or the problem that you solved or the format of the presentation? How does your writing enlighten your reader to think harder about your content, the world, and the writing?

By honing in on just what are the most vital elements of writing, one can create units that are more authentic to the real world. I don't see this as preparing them for a test; I see this as preparing them for something altogether more important: life.

But using strategies across the content areas is only one way to ensure that writing skills transfer. In order to help students transfer what they are learning from classroom to classroom is to also reflect on the quality of assessments themselves. After all, if the classroom tests don't connect with students, you will be hard-pressed to get a real sense of the depth of what they know. Therefore, we need to assess our own assessments.

After all, we may not have a lot of say in the quality of the Common Core assessments, but we can always adapt, revise, and improve our own classroom assessments to aid students in preparing for the CC tests.

If you are interested in pursuing more resources on 6 Traits writing, check out the following resources:

■ *Traits of Writing: The Complete Guide for Middle School*, Scholastic
■ *Daily Trait Warm-Ups: 180 Revision and Editing Activities to Kick Off Writing Time,* Scholastic.

Developing Meaningful Assessments and Prompts

Developing our own meaningful assessments is a key element in Common Core preparations. If CC is meant to be more aligned to real-life skills, for instance, then our classroom tests should be as well. And if life outside school demands some kind of writing every day, well then, perhaps our lessons, informal, and formal assessments should reflect that importance.

But remember, CC is only a guide across the ocean. You create the means to row the boat. And if your classroom assessments aren't meaningful, then you are down an oar.

I think meaningful assessments can come in many shapes and sizes. In fact, to be thoroughly engaging and to draw the best work out of the students, assessments should come in different formats. Thankfully, through project-based learning and interdisciplinary writing, we are looking at a more fluid future in testing formats. As long as the format itself is aligned with real-world skills, a meaningful assessment does not need to be lock step with a particular structure.

When I think about my own definition of a "meaningful assessment," I think of the following requirements:

1. The assessment must have value other than "because it's on the test."
2. It must have value to the individual student who is taking it.
3. It should have impact on the world beyond the student "self," whether it is on the school site, the outlying community, the state, country, world, etc.
4. It must incorporate skills that a student needs for his or her future, and those skills do not include how well they regurgitate facts about content.

To address these requirements, I developed the following guided questions:

1. Does the assessment involve project-based learning?
2. Does it allow for student choice of topics?
3. Is it inquiry-based?
4. Does it ask that students use some level of Internet literacy to find their answers?
5. Does it involve independent problem-solving?
6. Does it incorporate the 4Cs?
7. Do the students need to communicate their knowledge via writing in some way?
8. Does the final draft or project encourage a variety of other modalities in its presentation? (visual, oral, data, etc.)

Clearly not all assessments achieve every single characteristic listed above. But in our attempt to address some of these elements, we will have made our assessments so much more meaningful . . . even more so than those assessing the Common Core Standards. There, I said it. The Common Core tests, as it turns out, move towards a more meaningful assessment, but clearly they are not fully there yet.

One of the reasons they aren't meaningful is in how they, and other standardized tests, are utilized. The fact is that high-stakes tests were not meant to be high-stakes. They should and still can be a mere snapshot of ability that takes a back seat to the real learning and achievement going on in everyday assessments observed by the teacher.

The key here, however, is to use assessments formatively and assess every day so that students don't feel the assessments are summative simply because they are only whipped out at the ends of units or quarters. Assessments should be used formatively, but not in boring, multiple-choice daily quizzes. Rather, there should be more frequent informal assessments that take more than just a snapshot of a student's knowledge. They capture the information and, yes, data (which is not a bad word) on just how well a student functions and grows and learns.

I liken high-stakes testing to chronicling a recent landscaping job. Once the plants are in, a photo is snapped. Sure, work has happened, but is the landscaping at its most beautiful or lush? No. However, if you take pictures over a period of time, you are able to see the trees grow and the bushes bloom, and the vines crawl. It also allows you to retrain vines, cut back bushes, and manicure lawns to perfect the picture. And, here's the clincher: there's never a final snapshot, one that is meant to be evaluated for all time. Nope. What should be evaluated is how the landscaper adjusted the view throughout the year, not the final product, which is, frankly, always in progress.

So too is learning and assessing. Even at the end of the year, the "summative" assessments really should be used formatively and evaluated as a mere pausing point in someone's accomplishments, not the end-all determination of one's talent as a landscaper . . . or as a student.

But frankly, any assessment that sounds cool can still be made meaningless. It's how the students interact with the test that makes it meaningful. Remember the 4Cs and ask: does the assessment allow for:

- **Creativity**—Are the students creating or just regurgitating? Are they being given credit for presenting something other than what was described?
- **Collaboration**—Have they spent some time working with others to formulate their thoughts, brainstorm, or seek feedback from peers?
- **Critical thinking**—Are the students doing more work than the teacher in seeking out information and problem-solving? Is there an emphasis on the process of thinking over finding a single correct answer?
- **Communication**—Does the assessment emphasize the need to communicate the content well? Is there writing involved as well as other modalities? If asked to teach the content to other students, what methods will the student use to communicate the information and help embed it more deeply?

So as an activity for myself, I created a rubric to look at whenever I was wondering if an assessment was going to be a waste of time or was going to connect with the students. I thought I'd share it in Table 1.1.

Another way to ensure that an assessment is meaningful, of course, is to simply ask the students what they thought. Design a survey after each major unit or

TABLE 1.1 Rubric to Determine the Usefulness of an Assessment

Category	Ready to Implement	Rethink Purpose	Ditch this Assessment!
Creativity	Students are given a list of choices or unlimited choices of ways in which to display their knowledge	Gives students a limited number of choices (one to three) of ways to show their knowledge	Teacher/system-dictated format
Collaboration	Students are discussing and sharing throughout the assessment process	Students are permitted to discuss during the brainstorming portion of the activity only	No student discussion permitted at any stage of this assessment
Critical Thinking	Questions ask students to create, evaluate, and apply as well as analyze, remember, and understand. Students find or define problems themselves, and use skills to pose solutions	Questions are Costa's Level 2 or Bloom's Understand Level only. Students answer the prompt posed, but do not necessarily unearth the problem themselves	Questions are Costa's Level 1 or Bloom's Remember Level only. Students answer the prompt posed in the method being required
Communication	Insists on a variety of methods of communicating the content. Assesses the effectiveness of the communication method	Offers students a limited number of choices to communicate their knowledge. These methods are all or most of a particular modality. When assessing, weighs content over process	Uses only a single method of evaluation. Assesses content only

assessment. Or, better yet, if you want to encourage students to really focus on the requirements on a rubric, add a row that's only for them to fill out for you. That way, the rubric is more interactive for the students, and you get feedback on the assessment's level of meaningfulness as soon as possible. Not only does that give me quick feedback, but also that row becomes an outlet for the student that engages them in utilizing the rubric more fully. As an instructor and lesson designer, I want a quick turnaround between when I assign an assessment and knowing if I need to adjust the assessment to meet the needs of future learners. By also giving them their own row on the rubric to fill out, the students own the rubric even more, and will pay more attention to what I fill out knowing that I gave them an opportunity to also give me feedback. It's one way the students and I can learn reciprocally. Table 1.2 is an example of a quick rubric I designed for a general writing assessment.

TABLE 1.2 Quick Rubric for a General Writing Assignment

Category	4 Goes Beyond Assignment	3 Meets Expectations	2 Approaches	1 Does Not Even Come Close!
Ideas and Analysis	• Is full of original ideas to complement the content • Evidence is solid and backed up by quotes from the resources as well as outside sources and/or experiences • Addresses all parts of the prompt	• There are some original ideas in the analysis • There is evidence to back up original thought • Addresses most parts of the prompt	• Ideas are retell from resources • There is some evidence from resources • Attempts to address the prompt	• Content is not addressed • There is lack of evidence • Does not address the prompt
Writing Quality	• Sentence fluency and variety • High-level word choice beyond those used in the resources • Conventions are indicative of a final draft	• There is some sentence variety (perhaps using sentence stems echoing instructor's language) • Grade-level word choice (many found in resources) • Conventions indicate a solid draft	• Simple sentences with little or no variety • Low-level word choice • Conventions indicate a rough draft	• Low-level sentence structure with no variety • Low-level word choice that is also repetitive • Conventions are not grade-level and errors get in the way of the reader's comprehension
APA Format	• APA format is followed	• APA format is attempted	• Resources are listed but not in APA format	• There are no resources listed
Meaningful Assessment? (for student to fill out)	• This content of this assessment is meaningful to my learning • The method of delivery that is being asked is absolutely meaningful to the goals of my program	• Much of the content needed for this assessment is meaningful • The method of information delivery is potentially meaningful depending on my own effort	• The content learned for this assessment has little to do with the goals of my program • The method of information delivery may not be applicable to the goals of my program	• The content learned does not align with the goals of this program • The method of delivery is unrelated and meaningless to the goals of this program

Date Created: July 25, 2012

Of course, in addition to developing meaningful rubrics, which are invaluable when you are assigning and assessing writing quality, you should also have some quick tips in developing meaningful prompts.

In terms of developing a meaningful prompt, two key characteristics of a meaningful written assessment are whether the assignment is based in real life, and whether the student was given some modicum of choice. In the spirit of those two elements, one might look at the following:

Scientific professions: biologist, zoologist, marine biologist, astronaut, doctor, etc.

Historical professions: archeologist, archivist, art historian, etc.

Mathematical professions: engineer, accountant, economist, etc.

Combine these with the choice of product, and you might end up with a meaningful prompt for a written assessment.

> Imagine you are a _____. You (describe the profession). Write a (give a choice like newspaper article, lab report, brochure, diary entry, business letter, ad, etc.). In it, identify _____, analyze possible causes, and propose a solution.

But the most powerful way for students to really feel that an assessment is meaningful is if they themselves own the test and its expectations. After all, if the Common Core Standards are merely a guide, then why not involve the students in developing the manuals to achieve them in your classroom?

Student-Created Assessments and Rubrics

In my first book, 'Tween Crayons and Curfews: Tips for Middle School Teachers, I devoted a whole section to student-created rubrics and student-created assessments. I wanted to spend a little time here reviewing and expanding on those concepts.

Student-created assessments are a sure-fire way for students to connect with the material. The key is to teach students how to develop great, high-level questions. Since we know that great questions are actually evidence of deep comprehension, you can use the questions that students develop as a means to assess them in their content knowledge.

I like showing them Costa's Levels of Questions. It seems to me to be a more bite-sized version of Bloom's. For instance, I might show the students something like Table 1.3.

From there, I would teach students about the different forms of assessment questions: multiple-choice (which, by now, they are all experts in answering), true/false, rank order, short-answer, etc.

Once they have the swing of levels and formats, students can then begin to develop their own questions. To compile a student-created assessment I do the following:

TABLE 1.3 Costa's Levels of Questions

LEVEL 1: These questions ask students to recall, define, list, etc. This embeds information into short-term memory, but frankly, it may be lost over time.

LEVEL 2: These questions ask students to process and comprehend the information in a deeper way.

LEVEL 3: These questions ask students to create, evaluate, and judge. They require students to interact with the questions through prediction or hypothesis.

Topic	Level I *Define, list, count, recall, describe, identify*	Level II *Analyze, categorize, infer, compare, contrast, sequence*	Level III *Imagine, evaluate, judge, predict, create, speculate*
ELA	In the play *A Midsummer Night's Dream*, who ended up in love with Helena?	Use examples from the play to describe the theme proving that love is fickle.	Predict how your relationships would change if the threat of Puck's interventions were always present.
Math	Solve for x. 4x = 16	Use the Pythagorean Theorem to find the height of the flagpole, given that the shadow is 10 feet long and the hypotenuse is 25 feet.	What kind of growth will the world population see in the next ten years? Exponential growth or decay, linear growth or decay, zero slope, or a combination? Justify your response.
History	What amendment in the constitution gives the public the right to bear arms?	Compare and contrast today with the era in which the 2nd Amendment was included in the constitution.	If the 2nd Amendment were rescinded today, how might American society be changed?
Science	What is an X chromosome? What is a Y chromosome?	Compare and contrast the X and Y chromosome.	What do you know about chromosomes that can help you predict a trait in the birth of a child?
Spanish	Conjugate the verb, *tener* into past tense.	What are the similarities and differences between the informal and formal verbs in Spanish when addressing people of different ages?	Create a new Spanish verb ending in "er" and use it in five sentences.

1. Assign students to think of ten questions each based on your subject matter. Let them know that they have to develop questions of different levels and formats.

2. Have them each turn in their complete set of ten.

3. Cull the best questions to seed your own student-created assessment.

4. Assign students from one period to develop questions that become another period's quiz, or have small groups develop quizzes for each other.

Developing student-created rubrics takes a little more strategizing. In my last book, I wrote about a particular method of guiding students to develop classroom rubrics. I wrote about whole group or small group mini-lessons where students learned academic language by translating rubrics written in "teacher-ese." I permit students to translate rubrics into their own words so that they understand the expectations even more. I allow the students to have a hand in voting on the most comprehensible language they can think of to describe achievement. For instance, when you look back at Table 1.2, you can see the column, "Does Not Even Come Close!" This is actually an example from a rubric created by my third-period class. Period 4, on the other hand, designated that same column, "Epic Fail!" Customizing rubrics keeps students involved and on their toes, and if translated by them, students understand far more what is expected.

What I want to go into here is an expansion of that concept, this time with the students not only developing the language, but also setting the expectations for the assessment itself.

In this case, I want to take on one of the 4Cs. After all, it's difficult to assess "collaboration." So why not have the students help develop the rubric to do so?

1. In whole or small groups, have the students define what it means to collaborate.

2. Have them brainstorm what a teacher SEES when they see collaborating students.

3. Have them brainstorm what a teacher HEARS when they hear a collaborative group.

4. Keep a list of this brainstorm using quotes from the students themselves.

5. Use this language to seed the rubric for evaluating high-level collaboration.

In Table 1.4, you see the initial brainstorming list. Table 1.5 shows the list created into a more formal rubric designed by the students to assess "collaboration."

By having the students make the rules about what defines, excels, meets, and needs improvement in their own writing, they will be more likely to find value in the rubrics and the assessments being used in the classroom. And a written assessment that students understand is one that is a step closer to being more meaningful.

TABLE 1.4 Initial Brainstorming List on Collaboration

What does collaboration look like?	What does collaboration sound like?
"Kids working together"	"There's a buzz in the room"
"Kids leaning towards the center of the table"	"It's not silent, but if you pass the tables, everyone's talking about the topic"
"Students writing on one paper together"	"Appropriate disagreeing"
"A lot of nodding"	"Clapping"
	"Kids talking and then calling the teacher to come over"

TABLE 1.5 Rubric: How Well Are We Collaborating?

Category	3 The Whole Group Is Collaborating Well	2 Imbalanced Work Load/Not All Are on Task	1 Stalemate! No Work is Getting Done!
Evidence Seen	• Kids are working together • Kids are actively listening to each other • Kids all have their hands on one paper/project • Rules (read around, peer editing, etc.) are running smoothly	• Some kids are working together • Some students are doing their own thing • Some kids are choosing to do their own work without consulting others • It's taking a while to get the ball rolling	• The students are not communicating • The students are all doing their own thing • Students are not on task • There is a breakdown of rules and kids won't show each other their work
Evidence Heard	• All students get excited about the topic; it's like an eruption of appropriate noise • There is agreeing and disagreeing. Students are listening to each other before speaking	• Some students are discussing the topic • There are some interruptions, but overall, most students in the group are speaking	• Silence. Crickets. • Arguing. The group cannot come to a consensus or can't move on from a decision

2

Argument

The Universal Writing Genre

Mathematically proficient students understand and use stated assumptions, definitions, and previously established results in constructing arguments. They make conjectures and build a logical progression of statements to explore the truth of their conjectures. They are able to analyze situations by breaking them into cases, and can recognize and use counterexamples. They justify their conclusions, communicate them to others, and respond to the arguments of others.

(Common Core State Standards in Math)

The Argument for Argument

The reason that the Common Core State Standards focus so heavily on argumentation as a genre is because of its frequency of use in the world around us.

I mean, of course we see persuasion in ads: "Buy our new teeth whitening system, Enamel-off, and never worry about your teeth enamel again!" But obviously, it also exists in politics, law, sales, and more.

Even in my home life I hear really persuasive arguments from my 7-year-old when he begs to watch his favorite show. "Please let me watch *Ninjago*. I learn a lot about engineering from watching the Legos!" Yeah, right.

The fact is, you can't escape persuasive messaging. For those reasons, and others, we must help students recognize the ocean of good argument out there and the swamp of bad argument. We have to help them dive into the water themselves, and swim successfully in its depths.

This chapter will focus on how to teach the common features of an argument more effectively by providing examples of the kinds of assignments, assessments, and activities that different disciplines can do to meet these requirements. After all, just as writing is a universal subject, so is argument the universal genre.

Now, language arts has been teaching persuasive writing for lo' these many years. However, even they are now being asked to broaden their definition of what it is to persuade. We are now, instead, being asked to argue.

As an ELA teacher of persuasive writing, I have generally swung between asking students to write to prompts that are friendly and can be answered largely with a student's own personal experience, and those that require the more challenging expectation of comprehending a pro/con article.

For instance, in the past, we may have provided students with everything they needed to answer a simple yes/no question. Perhaps we gave the students a pro/con article from a grade-level appropriate magazine, one that has interviews on both sides of a single issue. Some sources for these articles that colleagues and I have used in the past were:

- Scholastic News
- Time for Kids
- NYTime Upfront.

Or even online sites or apps like:

- Pro/Con.org
- eLearnassignments.com.

We then asked students something like the following prompt:

> Do you believe that school cafeterias should serve more healthy foods? Write a persuasive essay that supports your point of view.

A yawn-of-a-prompt, to be sure. Clearly, many superficial questions, yes/no ones, are lower-level, and can be answered in a simple yes or no/pro or con response that require students to use evidence (either textual or personal experience) to back up their point of view.

However, this doesn't truly ask students to do the real questioning or to develop a take on a problem that is unique to their own research. It also doesn't ask them to look at things through a more complex lens or a different perspective. What if the issue isn't so black-and-white, as most issues are? Remember, we're trying to make assessment more authentic and meaningful (see Chapter 1), and by lowering the level of information a student must sift through to determine their own point of view, we are therefore stunting their ability to function outside of school. While the student must learn to take a stand on a point of view, the complexity of the text from which they formed their standpoint should now be, according to the Common Core, more rigorous and dense.

The Common Core Standards are meant to "ensure that students gain adequate exposure to a range of texts and tasks. Rigor is also infused through the requirement that students read increasingly complex texts through the grades."

This range of texts should be both qualitative and quantitative in nature, represented by selections based in all disciplines. And, no, as far as I'm concerned, the textbooks don't count as sufficient to use alone in one's research! I'm talking about excerpts and selections from pieces outside of school: of speeches by famous scientists, primary documents, and resources by historians, or even reviews of music or pieces of art.

Looking back at our typical persuasive essay prompt, we can now evolve this kind of argument into something completely different and higher-level. If we were to involve rigorous resources from which evidence should be culled, the resulting essay would be very different. For example, what if the prompt asked instead:

> Look back at a few of our recent articles that we read earlier this year. Read over the *Scholastic News* article on school litter and the *New York Times* upfront article on developing sustaining gardens in schools. Then, look again at the excerpt we read from Carl Hiaasen's *Hoot*. Using factual evidence from the articles, science facts from the young adult novel, your science textbook, and any other outside resources you wish to incorporate, develop an argument for how a school can build a 21st century learning environment for its students.

Genres: informational articles, op-ed pieces, young adult fiction, textbook, argumentation writing, narrative writing (because undoubtedly the student would have to use elements of concrete description in describing his or her 21st century school).

Academic vocabulary: article, sustaining, excerpt, factual evidence, resources, incorporate, develop, argument, environment.

Subjects integrated: reading, writing, science.

In other words, the Common Core methodology changes things greatly. In the past, we gave a single document from which to pull evidence and asked students, "Which side do you agree with?" (a cut-and-paste, black-and-white view of arguing). From here on in, the plan is to provide multiple pieces from different points of view and ask students, "What do you make of this topic?" It's a broader, more universal, and, yes, more authentic assessment of their ability to write and their ability to communicate content.

In fact, one can pull prompts from the real world itself using texts culled from the world around us. Better yet, allow students to find their own argumentation topics.

I recently read a piece from TheCreativityPost called "The Educational Value of Creative Disobedience." The piece stated that:

> In this age of innovation, even more important than being an effective problem solver, is being a problem finder. It's one thing to look at a problem and be able to generate a solution; it is another thing to be able to look at an ambiguous situation, and decide if there is a problem that needs to be solved.

I love this. I love that it's about making the kids work to find their own questions and their own answers, and it feeds directly into the challenges of teaching the Common Core method of argumentation. For it is no longer about feeding students both the problem and the solution, but making them aware that they have the power to both unearth issues that need solving and invent pathways towards setting solutions in motion.

I guess the way I see it, our job isn't to teach students the answers but, instead, to guide students to do the following:

1.   Discover a problem/issue/an important point of view to relay;

2.   Research possible solutions that do already exist and support one; or,

3.   Research enough that they can begin to use their expertise to trigger their own unique solutions;

4.   Begin down a road of advocacy, putting their thoughts into concrete movement so it doesn't simply remain static, on the page on which they declared their learning.

And all of this involves writing. All. Of. This. Involves. Writing.

And it isn't limited to language arts anymore. For argument is used in every discipline. After all, a scientist must defend their hypothesis before it becomes accepted as fact just as a historian must argue for funds to continue for another year of an archeological dig.

The Common Core Standards require that evidence-based argumentation writing be utilized in every subject.

> In fact, the Math standards ask that students be able to . . . "Construct viable arguments and critique the reasoning of others . . . Mathematically proficient students are also able to compare the effectiveness of two plausible arguments, distinguish correct logic or reasoning from that which is flawed, and . . . explain what it is."

What this might look like in a Common Core assessment is very different than prior assessments required. If we look at a typical math released question, you can see the rigor of not just the mathematical computation, but also the argument that is required to justify the computation. A prompt for an eighth grade math student may look something like the one shown in Figure 2.1.

But before we launch further into how every discipline can step-by-step their way towards integrating argumentation writing, let's dive a little deeper into the features of argumentation as a writing genre.

Features of Argumentation as a Writing Genre

First off, let's just touch on a little vocabulary so we're all on the same page here. Let's look at the issue of persuasive vs. argument. They are not one and the same. Check out the chart in Table 2.1, from the white paper written by Lauren Davis on "The 5 Things Every Teacher Should Be Doing to Meet the Common Core State Standards."

An engaging visual example of the difference can be viewed on YouTube in a little claymation movie called "How to Write a Persuasive Essay: An Introduction" by art teacher "Ms. Wilson."

Below you will see three different linear functions represented in three different ways.

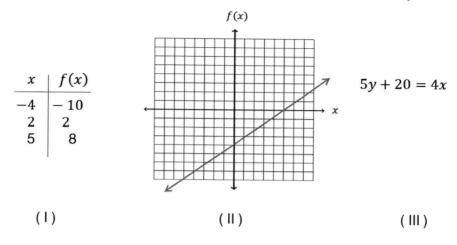

$$f(x)$$

x	$f(x)$
-4	-10
2	2
5	8

$$5y + 20 = 4x$$

(I)   (II)   (III)

Which function has the greatest rate of change? Do any pair of functions share the same rate? Justify your answer.

FIGURE 2.1

TABLE 2.1 Features of Persuasion vs. Argument

Genre	Definition	Common Features
Persuasion	Appeals to the emotions of the audience	Uses techniques such as bandwagon, plain folks, glittering generalities, name calling, and snob appeal
Argument	Appeals to logic and reason	Consists of a thesis/claim, evidence, concession/refutation, and a more formal style

The key difference here is that argument is more evidence-based while persuasion is more emotionally based. Certainly this means tweaking prompts, but perhaps, and more importantly, this also means a stress on research, text-based evidence, and transferring knowledge into writing to prove a point.

Life is full of the use of persuasive techniques, some of them quite effective, some of them rather cheap. After all, haven't we all read student essays built not on evidence but on tears, built not on proof but on mere well-written opinion? Good arguing takes real skill and knowledge of content. A lawyer doesn't just persuade a jury; she must provide an argument. A job applicant pitches himself as a potential employee, not by begging, but by presenting an argument for why he is the best suited for the job. A scientist competes for a grant not only by pulling on the heartstrings of the potential funder, but also by explaining the importance of such underwriting. A writer sells an idea in a query letter based on the facts that make that person the clear choice as a possible literary investment.

Another way to look at the importance between the differences in these topics is to look at real-world examples around us. Look at Figure 2.2.

It's important to note that there are essential persuasive elements that should exist in every piece of argumentation writing. Nevertheless, here is a short list of the components that, I believe, are essential elements for arguing in every discipline:

1. **The thesis statement/main topic sentence**—The thesis is the map of the essay. It not only states the argument but also gives an indication of the organization of the essay. All subjects must standardize the need to see one in a student's argument regardless of the content.

2. **Evidence**—Evidence is the quote, the computation, the data, the statistics, and the findings. Evidence backs up the argument made in the thesis statement. This is the content that the teacher as subject matter expert must verify. But it doesn't end there.

3. **Commentary**—Commentary is the original thought. It doesn't just translate the evidence to the layman; it brings in a new layer to the information, and that's what brings the argument home. Just make sure it isn't too emotional so that it crosses the line into mere persuasion. It must be fact- and evidence-based, not opinion-driven. (See Chapter 7 for more specific strategies on teaching commentary.)

So what does this look like in an essay that isn't focused on an ELA topic? How does a teacher who does not typically teach writing recognize the elements above? To answer that question, I have included a student sample from an interdisciplinary argumentation essay written by a student on a PE-related topic (Figure 2.3). I have indicated the elements above in order to help break down the argument you see into its basic building blocks. By looking at a possible example of the end result, one can then back-plan their lessons to meet these expectations.

Now, there are other components of course that you might recognize here:

■ Counterargument

■ Background information (context)

■ Transitions

FIGURE 2.2

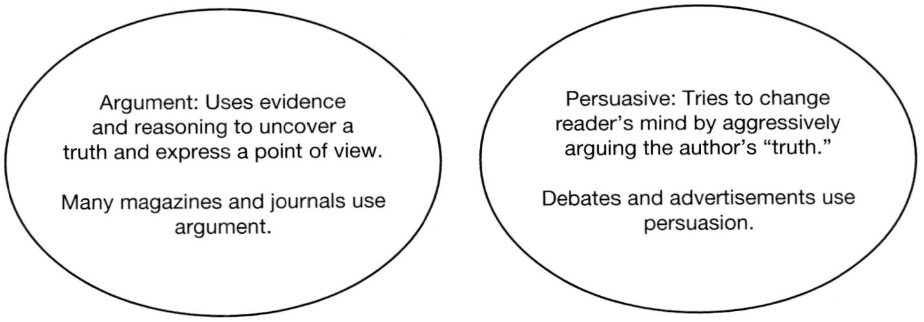

Argument: Uses evidence and reasoning to uncover a truth and express a point of view.

Many magazines and journals use argument.

Persuasive: Tries to change reader's mind by aggressively arguing the author's "truth."

Debates and advertisements use persuasion.

- Organization
- Word choice
- Conclusions, etc.

And these, I believe, must be taught in the ELA classroom. They are not, in my view, a part of the universal set of essential argumentation standards of writing that all disciplines should be asked to teach.

However, it's worth noting that even in math, a student should be able to provide evidence in a counterargument. They should be able to recognize that the other side isn't "crazy" and actually has a point. They should be able to define what makes another person's opinion valid in any content area.

Also, a teacher of any discipline should still hold students accountable for using good transitions, word choice, etc. I just don't believe that a science teacher should use instructional time to explicitly teach transition words that aren't related to the content. There is, after all, a line drawn somewhere. However, students must be held responsible for transferring what they are learning in ELA to other classroom subjects, and that comes with content-area teachers being aware of the elements that go into good writing.

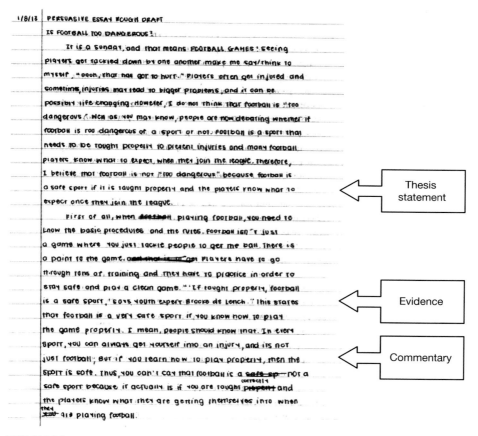

FIGURE 2.3A

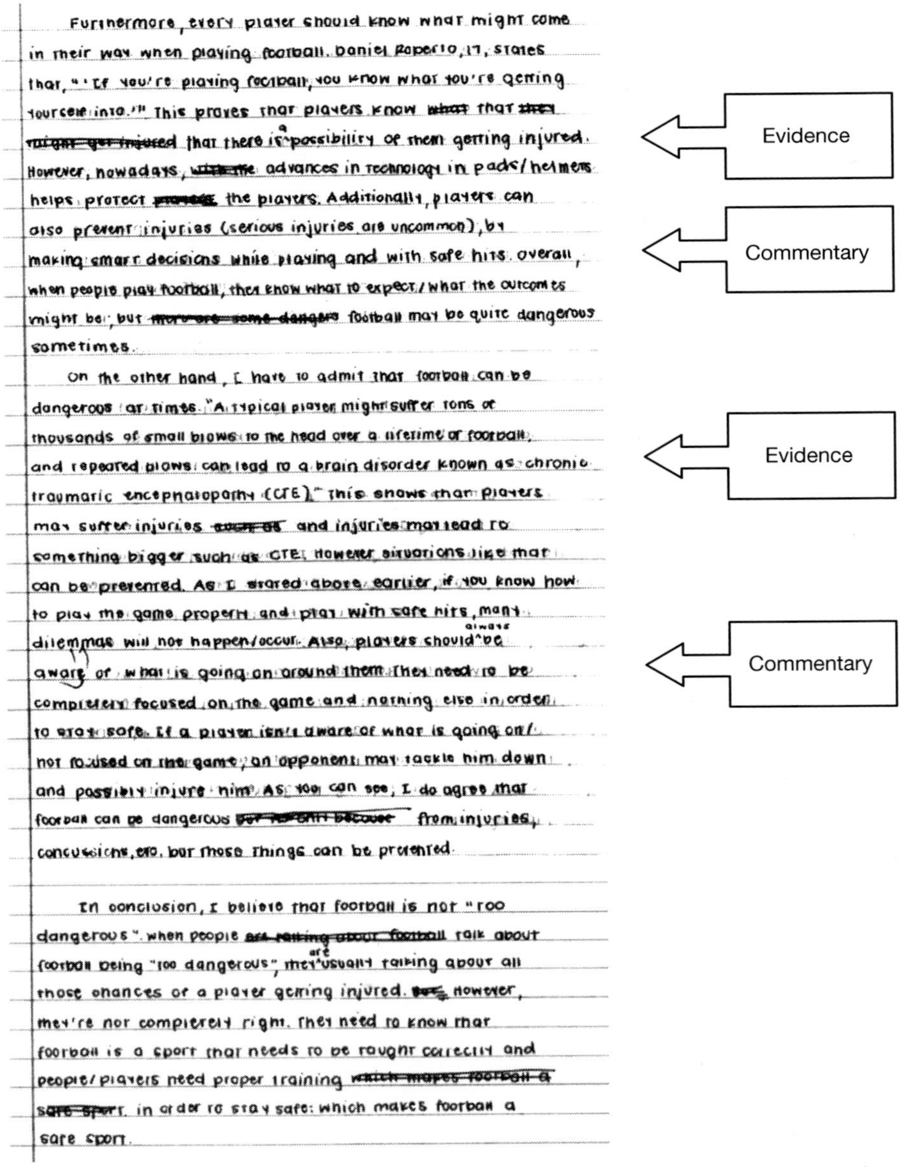
Furthermore, every player should know what might come in their way when playing football. Daniel Roperto, 17, states that, "'If you're playing football, you know what you're getting yourself into.'" This proves that players know ~~what~~ that ~~they might get injured~~ that there is a possibility of them getting injured. However, nowadays, ~~with the~~ advances in technology in pads/helmets helps protect ~~[illegible]~~ the players. Additionally, players can also prevent injuries (serious injuries are uncommon), by making smart decisions while playing and with safe hits. Overall, when people play football, they know what to expect/what the outcomes might be, but ~~there are some dangers~~ football may be quite dangerous sometimes.

On the other hand, I have to admit that football can be dangerous at times. "A typical player might suffer tens of thousands of small blows to the head over a lifetime of football, and repeated blows can lead to a brain disorder known as chronic traumatic encephalopathy (CTE)." This shows that players may suffer injuries ~~such as~~ and injuries may lead to something bigger such as CTE. However situations like that can be prevented. As I stated above earlier, if you know how to play the game properly and play with safe hits, many dilemmas will not happen/occur. Also, players should always be aware of what is going on around them. They need to be completely focused on the game and nothing else in order to stay safe. If a player isn't aware of what is going on/not focused on the game, an opponent may tackle him down and possibly injure him. As you can see, I do agree that football can be dangerous ~~but [illegible] because~~ from injuries, concussions, etc. but those things can be prevented.

In conclusion, I believe that football is not "too dangerous". When people ~~are talking about football~~ talk about football being "too dangerous", they are usually talking about all those chances of a player getting injured. ~~But~~ However, they're not completely right. They need to know that football is a sport that needs to be taught correctly and people/players need proper training ~~which makes football a safe sport~~ in order to stay safe; which makes football a safe sport.

FIGURE 2.3B

Therefore, if we can tease apart the most universal essential elements of argumentation from the additional ones saved for the language arts classes to assign and assess, think just how far we will have come in preparing our students for their future as argument experts regardless of the topic.

The good news is that, for many subjects, there are multiple structures that are acceptable from which teachers and students can choose. There is not a hard-and-fast rule that says, "This is the absolute only way you can write argument." We explore just some of the choices in the next section of this chapter.

Possible Structures of Cross-Curricular Argumentation Essays

The structure of an argument essay is important because the reader can't be persuaded if he or she is struggling to follow the logic or sequence of what is being argued.

Prior to assigning students to write the actual essays, it might be wise, at least in the beginning, to get them using graphic organizers like one found on the ReadWriteThink website. You can assign an organizer as homework and have them fill it in on their own time to bring in before they make formal arguments either verbally or in writing.

You can also provide students with fill-in-the-blank options. For instance, you can give them this kind of activity when they learn how to write a thesis statement for your subject matter. Remember, it's a scaffold. That is, it serves to help them strengthen their writing, and then it can be pulled away once the student understands the structure and rationale of writing thesis statements in the first place.

A couple of argumentation thesis statement frames might be:

1. I strongly believe _____ because (reason #1) and (reason #2). *(And since the thesis statement is the map for the overall essay, Reasons 1 and 2 then become the order of the body paragraphs.)* Figure 2.4 is a student sample of a thesis statement, written on a science-related topic, that follows this format.

2. By examining _____, we can see _____, which many readers/students/ researchers, etc., don't see; this is important because _____.

In terms of providing writing scaffolds of overall essay structure, I've included a number of outlines that could be the basis of any argument, regardless of the subject

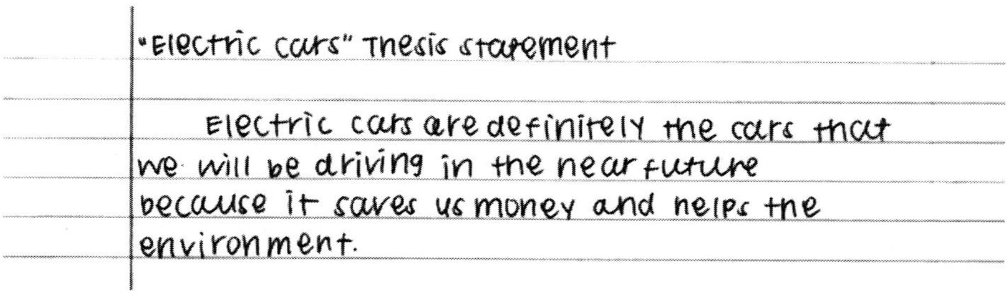

> "Electric cars" Thesis statement
>
> Electric cars are definitely the cars that we will be driving in the near future because it saves us money and helps the environment.

FIGURE 2.4

43

that fills in the content. I've included a student sample so that you can see how the outlines fill out once they get content and some decent writing strategies inserted.

This is my typical outline I use for the multiple paragraph argumentation essay. It breaks down each paragraph quite explicitly, so for all you ELA teachers or history teachers out there, this one might be for you:

I. Introduction
    A. Hook
    B. Background information
    C. Who is affected by this issue?
    D. Thesis statement
       1. Opinion + Reason #1 + Reason #2
       For instance: I strongly believe that we should be permitted to drink water in class because it is proven to help our brains remain more alert and will help improve our overall physical health.

II. Body paragraph: Reason #1
    A. Main topic sentence (general statement)
    B. Expands on the main topic sentence (gets more specific)
    C. Textual evidence
       1. Quote
       2. Statistic
       3. Data
       4. Personal experience.
    D. Commentary/connection to the evidence
    E. Transition to next paragraph.

III. Body paragraph: Reason #2
    A. Main topic sentence (general statement)
    B. Expands on the main topic sentence (gets more specific)
    C. Textual evidence
       1. Quote
       2. Statistic
       3. Data
       4. Personal experience.
    D. Commentary/connection to the evidence
    E. Transition to next paragraph.

IV. Counterargument
    A. Main topic sentence (states the opposing side's *best* point)
    B. Expands
    C. Textual evidence
    D. Commentary/connection
    E. Conclusion that *refutes* this point (i.e. why it's not enough to convince you).

V. Conclusion
   A. Reiterate thesis (uses different words)
   B. Solution/call to action.

Figure 2.5 is an example of a student argumentation essay that takes a side on the issue of violent video games.

But you certainly don't need a traditional five-paragraph essay in order to qualify for an argument. In fact, I would debate that argument uses all kinds of formats, and every teacher that includes argumentation in his or her lessons, units, or assessments can, and should, mix it up. The paragraphs can vary in length. Sometimes, all one needs for an informal assessment, in fact, is an argumentation statement. Frankly, that's the first step towards a more formal thesis statement, so why not require students to create an exit card comprised of a single sentence? However, if you're looking for some more formal possibilities, here are a couple more outlines that still highlight the skill of argumentation writing.

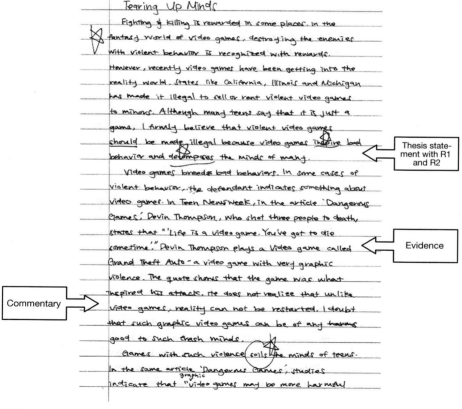

FIGURE 2.5A

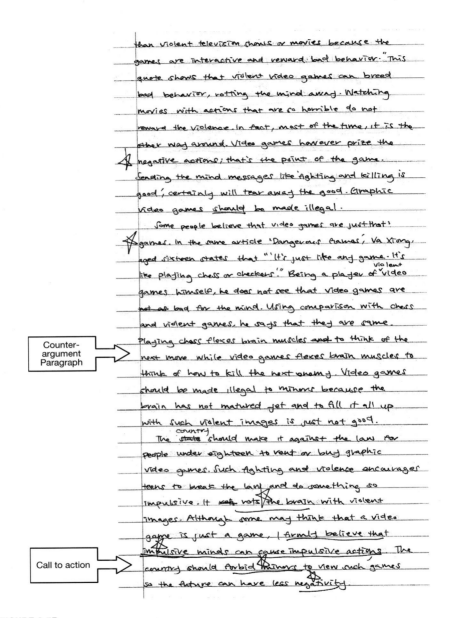

than violent television shows or movies because the games are interactive and reward bad behavior." This quote shows that violent video games can breed bad behavior, rotting the mind away. Watching movies with actions that are so horrible do not reward the violence. In fact, most of the time, it is the other way around. Video games however prize the negative actions; that's the point of the game. Sending the mind messages like 'fighting and killing is good', certainly will tear away the good. Graphic video games should be made illegal.

Counter-argument Paragraph →

Some people believe that video games are just that: games. In the same article 'Dangerous Games', Va Xiong, aged sixteen states that "'It's just like any game. It's like playing chess or checkers.'" Being a player of violent video games himself, he does not see that video games are not as bad for the mind. Using comparison with chess and violent games, he says that they are same. Playing chess flexes brain muscles and to think of the next move while video games flexes brain muscles to think of how to kill the next enemy. Video games should be made illegal to minors because the brain has not matured yet and to fill it all up with such violent images is just not good.

The state country should make it against the law for people under eighteen to rent or buy graphic video games. Such fighting and violence encourages teens to break the law and do something so impulsive. It rots the brain with violent images. Although some may think that a video game is just a game, I firmly believe that impulsive minds can cause impulsive actions. The

Call to action →

country should forbid minors to view such games so the future can have less negativity.

FIGURE 2.5B

This next one is a great single-paragraph possibility for any subject to use in a short-answer format that still fulfills many of the essential obligations for argument:

I. Introduction (think of this as a main topic sentence)
II. Body
    A. First point and supporting info
    B. Second point and supporting info
    C. Third point and supporting info.
III. Conclusion (think of this as a concluding sentence).

Here is yet another multiple-paragraph example:

I. Introduction (this states your thesis as well as the main point of why someone disagrees with you)
II. Body
    A. A statement of your overall point of view
    B. First point and supporting evidence
    C. Counterargument and supporting evidence
    D. Rebuttal and supporting evidence
    E. Second point and supporting evidence
    F. Counterargument and supporting evidence
    G. Rebuttal and supporting information.
III. Conclusion.

There are also outlines that have proven themselves to be used for specific subjects. For instance, there's the official outline for a scientific argument. Look at it in Figure 2.6.

Marsha Ratzel, an award-winning middle school science teacher from Kansas and a member of the Teacher Leaders Network, incorporates writing into many of her daily lessons. She says that,

> almost everything we have involves writing of some sort. In science, it's writing to explain and it's a very precise kind of writing . . . Science writing is more about what happened and the analysis of that. It's finding a conclusion you think you can explain and using evidence/data to back up what you said.

The outline above supports that goal.

Indeed, the fact is that the scientific argument contains many of the same elements that the other outlines possess, but in a streamlined format using the

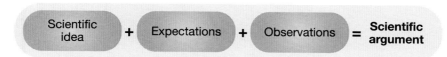

FIGURE 2.6

language of the content. Arthur Applebee believes that "'Generic' writing skills—ones that can be learned in English class and applied everywhere else—just won't do." He goes on to say that "Teachers of science (as well as of history and other subjects) need to help students write in the ways appropriate to their own subject areas." I agree that all teachers need to help students write, and by helping I don't simply mean assigning. But I still contend that the difference in expectation from subject to subject corrupts some level of transference between classrooms. I believe if we spoke more universally from subject to subject, transfer and writing growth across the disciplines would be improved. Therefore, don't ditch the content-area specific vocabulary, but instead additionally embed a more universal expectation for certain elements of writing in every classroom.

Think of it from a different perspective. In all actuality, a simple way to teach argument could also state:

Main Topic + Analysis + Evidence = Any Argument

My thought is that this boiled-down version should actually guide the development of a school-wide universal writing rubric that all subjects must use to assess the quality of communication that a student employs to describe any content.

Regardless of which outline you chose to have students complete, they have accomplished the task of communicating their content to you and their readers. As a teacher, it then becomes your task to give them a score based on both their knowledge of the subject (can be weighted greater if you prefer) and their ability to communicate that content through writing.

A Brief Note on Scoring Arguments

However, there is pushback from other content areas and teachers in fields other than language arts. It comes from the legitimate concern of scoring. How does a teacher who teaches science hold students accountable for writing quality in addition to content? Doesn't this increase the time spent grading? And how does one feel comfortable assessing writing when one doesn't know what's been taught and what the expectations are for that student?

That's where a simple, universal rubric comes in. That's also where creative scoring comes in.

Look at the mathematical paragraph in Figure 2.7. In it, a seventh grade student has selected an equation from one of those in their homework to justify why the equation solves what it does. Using the simple rubric and the two boxes in Figure 2.7, fill out the score for the student based on your knowledge of the content and communication.

What did you score the paragraph? The original teacher scored it a 5 in content and a 4 in writing. After all, where's the commentary? The original thought or connection to the world outside of school? Where's the persuasive word choice that takes a simple summary or explanation into the realm of argument? Nevertheless, that's a 9/10 total. That's the score that went into the grade book for this informal, formative assessment. It was accomplished with a quick skim and

I believe that the pythagorean theorem is ~~true~~ true because of the various mathematical proofs that back it up. I have seen over 90 different proofs, and I have proved a few of them myself. The first proof I saw, consisted of two squares, it looked sort of like this:

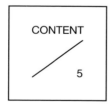 

In this particular proof, the large square represents $(a+b)^2$ because the length of one side is $a+b$. When squared, using properties of algebra, $(a+b)^2 = a^2 + 2ab + b^2$. The square on the right. The "ab" rectangles in that square are ~~the~~ each double the triangles in the first square. If you subtract the extra area of the triangles you are left with "c^2" o/ in mathematical terms $(a^2 + 2ab + b^2) - 2ab = a^2 + b^2 = c^2$. Thus proving the Pythagorean Theorem.

CONTENT	WRITING
/ 5	/ 5

Possible Universal Writing Rubric

1 = present
0 = not included/not grade level

Main Topic
Sentence
Evidence
Commentary
Conclusion
Conventions
(Spelling, Punctuation, Grammar)

FIGURE 2.7

a mere judgment of writing quality. And from a student's point of view, it doesn't take many times of being assessed in both writing and content to realize that he or she is going to be held accountable for communication quality in all classes.

The art of writing argument is a key that unlocks a world of possibilities. It is a skill that we see at every stage of life, from writing the inevitable cover letter to one day hopefully writing a letter of recommendation.

Cross-Curricular Activities and Assignments

In life, everything requires some kind of argument. Therefore, in school, every problem, every subject, and every task should come from that perspective as well. School must reflect the world around it, and argumentation is a key skill for college and career readiness regardless of the path a student takes.

If you look through the Common Core Standards, you'll see words peppered all over the place that point to the need to inject argumentation into every subject matter: "interpret," "argument," "analyze." It's about teaching students about a concept, helping them to sift through the plethora of resources out there, encouraging them to take a stand based on the evidence that they believe is the best, and requiring them to produce an argument that justifies their findings.

Sometimes, it just starts with a targeted conversation in each class at the beginning of the school year to set the tone that "Writing counts in every subject, in every room." Marsha Ratzel reiterates that:

> at the beginning of the year [assessing writing] is mostly formative. Lots of posing a question, letting them draft something and then sharing those drafts with each other. We'll read aloud answers . . . and let anyone change what they've written if they hear something better or they see an idea that they think they could incorporate. Lots of erasing and re-writing. We sort of build a common understanding (which I try to formalize into a rubric/checklist of sorts) of what is high quality writing. We use those as look-for's as we discuss . . . [with] a document camera, I could display their writing as they read it aloud. That worked great.

And setting up that expectation ahead of time saves a lot of time and heartache later when the actual assessed writing begins to arrive in your Inbox.

It is a process that writing teachers have been using forever, and it's a process that science, math, history, electives, heck, even PE, need to be adopting now.

For instance, take math. Rather than merely solving a math problem by having the equation serve as the answer in itself, the requirement to integrate argumentation writing will instead require a student to select the formula to use, take a stand on their proposed equation and solution, and use the computations as evidence to back up that argument. It is a multi-genre writing assessment that incorporates writing with quantitative evidence.

On the other side of campus, in the English language arts department, we are already spinning literary analysis into a literary argumentation composition in order to address the future of this more meaningful writing. Rather than teach two compartmentalized writing genres—persuasive during one quarter and literary analysis in another—doesn't it make more sense to blend the two and have the student *convince* the reader of the theme or the character change or the author's intent? Using more persuasive word choice and more targeted evidence, a student can morph a dry analysis into an argument for literary elements within a work. It comes at analysis from a different, more authentic angle, and it weaves argument into response to literature.

But sometimes it's difficult to imagine how to use something in your classroom without seeing models from which to learn. For this reason, I've divided the next section of this chapter into some different disciplines, giving examples of assessments that incorporate writing as well as some student samples.

Erik Burruss, a great math teacher from Los Angeles, CA, always has his math students justify their findings in a dual-entry journal (see more on dual-entry journals in Chapter 7). This method of pre-writing is, from here, easily converted to a more formal justification argument. Figure 2.8 is an example of a dual-entry journal that can then serve as a pre-write for a more formal argument.

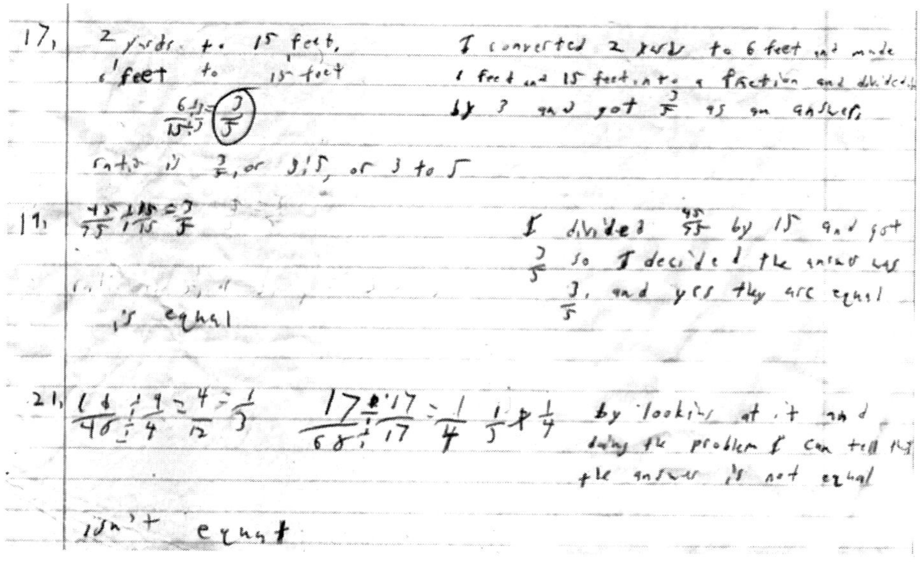

FIGURE 2.8

Science

Bear with me here. Earlier in this chapter I discussed a little about scientific argument, but I'm going to use science content to actually bring up a different point entirely in this section: that, in fact, argument can even be found embedded in other genres. As I've written before, there are expository scientific arguments; but argument can also be found in the most surprising of places. For instance, in Figure 2.9, there are elements of argument in the Edgar Allen Poe sonnet, "Sonnet—To Science." Even simply recognizing argumentation writing using the facts from one's discipline is valuable. In this case, the sonnet makes the argument that science has battled and won against legend and myth.

Science! True daughter of Old Time thou art!
Who alterest all things with thy peering eyes.
Why preyest thou thus upon the poet's heart,
Vulture, whose wings are dull realities?
How should he love thee? Or how deem thee wise,
Who wouldst not leave him in his wandering
To seek for treasure in the jeweled skies,
Albeit he soared with an undaunted wing?
Hast thou not dragged Diana from her car?
And driven the Hamadryad from the wood
To seek a shelter in some happier star?
Hast thou not torn the Naiad from her flood,
The Elfin from the green grass, and from me
The summer dream beneath the tamarind tree?

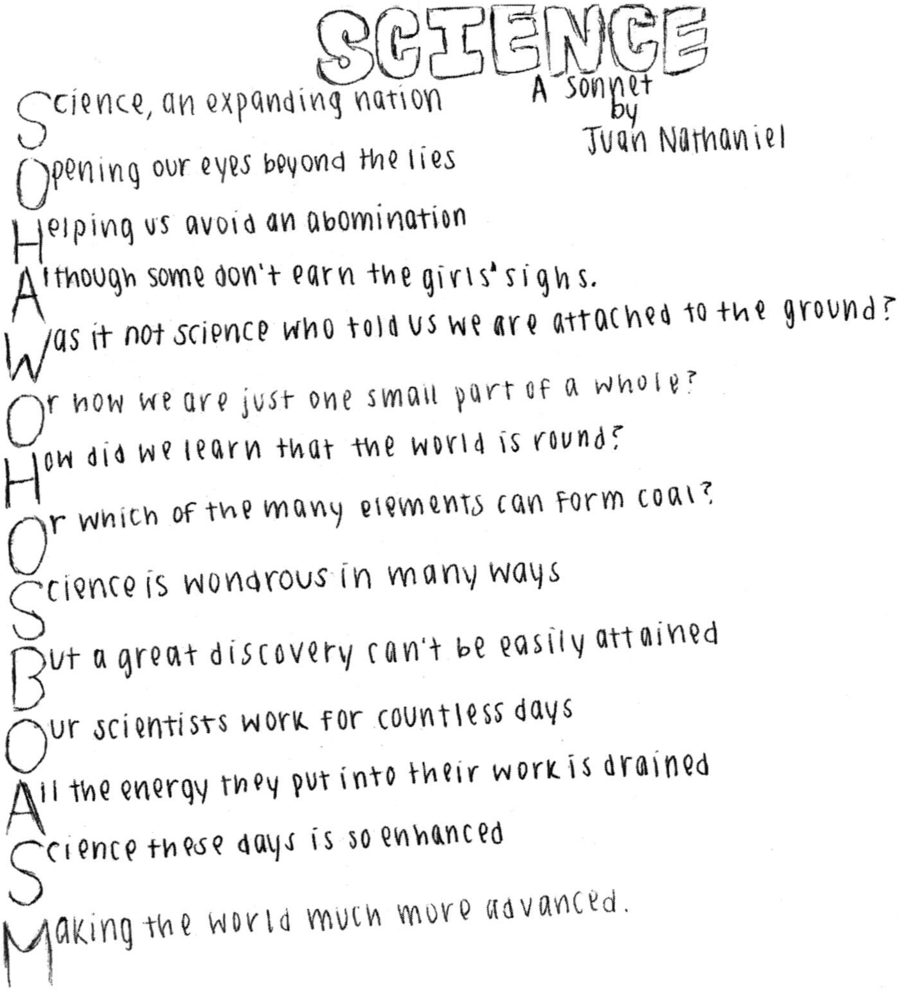

SCIENCE
A sonnet
by
Juan Nathaniel

Science, an expanding nation
Opening our eyes beyond the lies
Helping us avoid an abomination
Although some don't earn the girls' sighs.
Was it not science who told us we are attached to the ground?
Or how we are just one small part of a whole?
How did we learn that the world is round?
Or which of the many elements can form coal?
Science is wondrous in many ways
But a great discovery can't be easily attained
Our scientists work for countless days
All the energy they put into their work is drained
Science these days is so enhanced
Making the world much more advanced.

FIGURE 2.9

52

Do I really believe a science teacher needs to have their students mimic a Poe poem? Of course not. But I do believe that if we are talking about transferring knowledge from classroom to classroom, it's valuable when you stumble on an example, to show students the kinds of writing in which your content might be embedded. In this case, in a strange sort of way, we could be talking about a poetic argument. Or, perhaps, an argumentative poem?

Nevertheless, for those interested in tackling this kind of written assignment, you might have students do the following:

1. Ask the students to read the poem and identify the point of the argument.
2. Further identify the science that, according to the poem, preyed upon each preconceived concept that was mentioned.
3. Using the classical sonnet structure (fourteen lines with a couplet at the end), have the students compose their own scientific-argument sonnet.

The resulting science-sonnet might look like what you see in Figure 2.9 or 2.10.

Science Sonnet 1621

We laugh upon those before us

Whose ideas clearly myth;

But our grandson's sons will make quite a fuss

When they disprove our theories with

Their fancy gadgets and science nick-nacks

Even we won't understand.

Now, the world is round and there are some facts

Supporting this knowledge of land,

But when the earth was flat

You could fall right off

even the dumbest of people knew that.

At our ideas future generations certainly will scoff,

So why is it that this so called "truth"

Keeps changing more with science's youth?

FIGURE 2.10

History

Rod Powell, an award-winning high school social studies teacher and member of the Center for Teaching Quality, speaks about using a blended approach to writing in his classroom. Since the writing he sees outside of school seems to reflect narrative, argumentation, and informational writing, he brings that expectation into the classroom in a multi-genre way (see Chapter 6 on multi-genre writing). He also assesses his students using a writing rubric.

Many of his assignments seem to reflect the need to argue. In one assignment, he asks students to write a song about the Black Death and to then convince him, the mythical music mogul, that the song will sell. He insists that students write using a thesis statement and evidence. They also must include proper attribution of sources. Powell integrates writing, and specifically the art of writing argument, into his lessons on a daily basis.

ELA

In terms of ELA, there are countless ways to assess the common core in an uncommon way that fulfills the requirement for argumentation. Just as one example, I have students create book trailers to promote their current literature or even as an argument to read their own original narratives. This is just one example of how one can combine both literary analysis and argument much like what I wrote about earlier in this chapter.

A book trailer is much like a movie trailer in that it is a digital project that normally includes visuals and music to support persuasive text. The student must understand the content, of course: sequence, plot, suspense, characters, theme, etc. The students must also understand the structure of this method of communication: editing, inserting text, selecting music to complement the tone of the piece, and recording or simply uploading visuals.

Apple makes it very easy using their iPads because by using the iMovie app, one can just create a book trailer using the Book Trailer template. Of course, as a teacher, you need to see the text ahead of time so you can see just what the student plans to write to pitch the piece.

I ask the students to list, in a bulleted format, the lines of text (dialogue or otherwise) that are being planned in order to persuade a viewer to read the book/ short story.

So if a student were reading *The Boy in the Striped Pajamas*, she might create a list of text that uses argument that might look something like this:

Based on True Events
Every Friendship Has a Story
But This One's Different From the Rest
During the Holocaust
Two Friends From "Different Sides of the Fence"
Create a Bond that Can't be Broken
If You See Any Movie This Summer
This is the One
Come See The Boy in the Striped Pajamas.

Electives

Speech and debate—As a speech and debate electives teacher (as well as an ELA teacher), I often incorporate argument writing in my curriculum. Putting aside the necessary persuasive writing that debaters must accomplish for a structured competition, even those students competing in simpler speech categories must engage in argumentation. One assignment I have my students do every quarter is to pitch me the speeches they want to work on. They do this in the form of a short argument essay using the structure of a business letter:

Dear Mrs. Wolpert-Gawron:

During this quarter, I would like to enter the Oratorical Interpretation category. I worked very hard last quarter, and while I didn't place, I did improve a lot over the course of the 9 weeks. For that reason, I would like to select a specific speech for this next upcoming tournament.

If you notice my grades, I earned an A on my memorization test and I also earned an A 4 weeks later when I was tested on my ability to take direction and grow. I also am really interested in a particular speech, "Will Ferrell's Harvard Commencement Day Speech." I'm a big Will Ferrell fan, but I assure you, Mrs. W, that I will make it my own. I know that there are other students that want to compete with this speech, but if given the opportunity, I will show you that I will work on it harder than anyone. I know when it needs to be funny, and I know when it needs to be serious like in the part when he recites Shakespeare. Actually, it's never really serious. In fact, the Shakespeare he recites is really fake and he's made up his own Old English stanza (see, I've already studied it on my free time!). However, the speech does become serious in a sarcastic way, and as you know by my own dry humor in class, I have what it takes to really do this speech well.

I hope you will consider me for the Will Ferrell speech. I won't let you (or Will) down!

Sincerely,

In addition, students can indicate the elements of argument in different speeches that they are working on. Students participate in an informal argumentation assignment where they must recognize when (and how) a speaker is trying to persuade the audience.

I first introduce students to different forms of argument traps (see Table 2.2, reprinted from my last book).

Then they apply these techniques and others they recognize to the different speeches to analyze. From a speaking point of view, the kind of argument they identify sometimes gives them an indication of the tone in which they should be speaking. From a Common Core standpoint, I've incorporated argument into a forensics category that wouldn't normally involve anything but performance.

TABLE 2.2 Argument Writing Traps

Argument to the Man (*Ad Hominem*)—attacking the person rather than the point

Argument of Generalization—attacking a whole group

Needling—poking at your opponents simply to make them mad

Scare Tactics—freaking out your audience with scary scenarios as a means to make a point

Generalization—assuming what's generally true must always be true

Oversimplification—boiling down the topic too much

Appeal to Vehemence—just being plain loud or yelling over your opponent

Cyclical Reasoning—your argument is used as its own proof

Cliché—using the slogan on a bumper sticker as proof

Bandwagon—because so many people do it, or did it, it must be good evidence

Pigheadedness—just plain-old stubborn

Non Sequitur—what?! The dots are not connected.

Error of Fact—warning: one error generally means there are others. An audience loses faith in the author when it hears a factual error

Failure to State—taking no side or wavering in your position

Uninformed Opinion—there's no evidence. The debater doesn't back up their opinion with fact

Two Wrongs Make a Right—just because one side did it does not justify that the other side should

Let's take Tom Hank's speech, "The Power of Four," as an example. Figure 2.11 is an excerpt from the actual speech. My student has annotated on the speech, identifying the argumentation techniques and elements of good writing throughout.

PE

This kind of annotation exercise can be done in any classroom using any piece of text. For instance, here is a statement from Lance Armstrong's website denying the recent doping allegation from 2012. A portion of it reads:

Lance Armstrong Responds to USADA Allegation

I have never doped, and, unlike many of my accusers, I have competed as an endurance athlete for 25 years with no spike in performance, passed more than 500 drug tests and never failed one. That USADA ignores this fundamental distinction and charges me instead of the admitted dopers says far more about USADA, its lack of fairness and this vendetta than it does about my guilt or innocence.

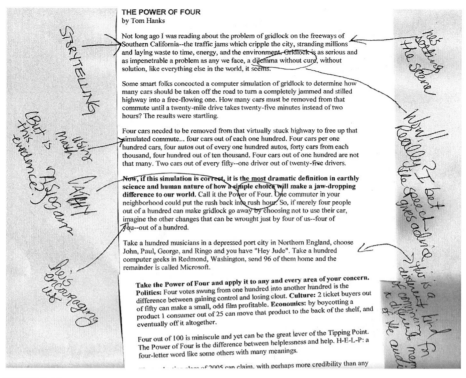

FIGURE 2.11

A student can highlight the persuasive words, circle the point of the argument, and even write a follow-up to the piece itself after doing research on doping allegations in other sports as well.

The point is to surround students with argument in every class so that they can't escape recognizing it and can't escape developing the skills to use it well.

Of course, once you have designed an assessment for the students, the key is to assess it yourself to ensure that it is a meaningful assessment. (See Chapter 1 for a rubric on meaningful assessing.) Besides the actual design and choice of prompt, another way to do that is in asking students to share their point of view with others once they have done their research and constructed their argument. Find ways to transfer their knowledge of a topic by introducing students to methods of getting their arguments out and seen by the world at large. After all, their research may be valuable to others. Their efforts and writing and opinions may help change their world. Allow them to utilize websites like You Decide that permits readers to vote on an issue. Students can then utilize their resulting tables and data in their writing. So, not only does their point of view help to drive the data, the tables and charts that result in their online participation can be used as evidence for their own argument. The more you bridge the outside world with what you are doing within the walls of your own classroom, the more meaningful the material and the more buy-in from the students.

More buy-in equates to better classroom management, and better classroom management helps towards student achievement. It's not a circle of life, but a circle of learning. They all blend together, as do the genres of writing themselves.

I wrote earlier in this chapter how argument now finds itself blending into every subject and every genre: literary analysis, historical speeches, scientific journals, etc. More specifically, and importantly for many content areas, it blends greatly with the standards for informational writing. They are like two great tastes that go great together. The blurring of the two genres is now more complex and more sophisticated than ever before when they were separated as individualized, categorized genres. (See Chapter 6 for more on multi-genre writing.)

From where I stand, argument brings the voice and the purpose to the informational writing. Informational writing brings the cohesive presentation of evidence and the synthesis of research to the argument.

So without further ado, let's launch into more detail about informational writing. For more information on teaching the art of argument writing, check out the following resources:

- *Teaching Argument Writing, Grades 6–12: Supporting Claims with Relevant Evidence and Clear Reasoning* by George Hillocks Jr.
- *Questions, Claims, and Evidence: The Important Place of Argument in Children's Science Writing* by Lori Norton-Meier, Brian Hand, Lynn Hockenberry, and Kim Wise.
- *Teaching Students to Write Argument (Dynamics of Writing Instruction)* by Peter Smagorinsky, Larry R. Johannessen, Elizabeth Kahn, and Thomas McCann.

3

Informational

It's All Around Us

> Write informative/explanatory texts to examine a topic and convey ideas, concepts, and information through the selection, organization, and analysis of relevant content.
>
> (Common Core Standards)

Informational writing is where we get down to the nitty-gritty of the changes in store for the Common Core world. It is a world that exemplifies nonfiction reading and writing. It is a world where science dominates science fiction. Or does it?

The fact is: humans are amazing. Without dreaming and writing and creating science fiction, there would be no science. Across the curricular aisle, one can also say that without historical fiction there would be fewer people appreciating the significance of our historical past.

So why is it so daunting to integrate both? Why can't a teacher promote both informational and narrative, both fiction and nonfiction? The fact is that they can. All teachers, no matter the subject matter, should be encouraging, promoting, and demanding students to be able to communicate their understanding of information using multiple methods.

Students should leave K12 education being able to pitch, demonstrate, explain, and inform using methods that include but are not limited to: podcasting, reader's theater, mock job interviews, oral idea pitches, news broadcasts, etc.

And these all start in writing.

So how does a teacher promote the communication of informational writing regardless of his or her content area? That's what this chapter will focus on. Here I will share lessons and exemplars that promote nonfiction work and ways a student can communicate what they know about the Common Core Standards.

Utilizing project-based learning, my unit that incorporates TED.com seems like a great place to introduce to you different strategies and activities to promote informational writing. It is a unit rich with different activities, strategies, and assessments that use the creation of a written TED-esque speech as the vessel to house these different assignments. Check out Appendix A to see the actual checklist of assignments for this unit. In this chapter, however, I will give you the gist of the unit, but then break it down into its parts so that you might incorporate its building blocks into any informational writing curriculum. Use the whole unit or its mini-assessments to build up any informational unit for any subject matter.

The TED Unit

The TED unit is one of the most intensive curricular packages I've designed (and because it also incorporates multiple genres of writing, you can see Chapter 6 for more on this topic). Based on the wonderful TED archive of speeches, it's an advocacy unit based on topics student groups get to select themselves. In other words, small groups might select a science-based advocacy topic (perhaps something on the environment or space travel). Small groups might also select something related to politics. The topics in the room range based on the interests of the students, and those interests represent multiple content areas.

What that means is that I am not the expert in the content of each and every project, but I am the guide in how to present the information the students must present. It's exciting for them to learn about because they have ownership in the selection of the topics, and it's exciting for me because it permits me to learn from them as much as they learn from me. That way, I'm not the only teacher in the classroom and they aren't the only learners. My job, as I see it, is to also model a joy in learning. I chose to go into more detail on this one particular unit because, when broken down into its parts, it contains many activities and strategies a teacher can use in any content area to promote writing and communicating in any subject matter.

I'm a big believer in checklists. I really believe in my own transparency so that students aren't in the dark as to what I will expect and why. Checklists also help me know where I want to go and how. I always set up a checklist at the top of each unit that I hand out to students so that they can:

1. Make sense of the big picture of a particular unit;
2. Share what they are doing with their parents or guardians so that there aren't mixed messages coming home regarding the purpose or pacing of assignments;
3. Help develop better time management skills by planning and prepping assignments in advance.

The cover sheet of my TED unit is meant to inform all stakeholders (students, parents, and myself) of the intention of the unit. If you want to see a checklist of assignments and key deadlines that were due over the course of this unit, see Appendix A.

We start the unit by watching some key videos throughout the first quarter, and I've been asking simple questions like: "What's the theme?" "Where did she get this idea?" "What is the call to action he is asking his audience to do?" The students take notes based on the evidence in the videos. (To see examples of students' note-taking from the TED videos, see Chapter 6.) Unbeknown to the students, we've been casually analyzing the informational speeches that we have watched. Analysis is a form of informational writing.

Before long, the students begin to identify that there are speech patterns many of the TED speeches possess regardless of whether they cover topics based in science or on art. It doesn't matter. Many of the presentations, regardless of the length, whether they are three minutes or twenty-three minutes, tend to share some key common traits like:

1. Hook
2. Background information
3. Narrative/memoir
4. Cited evidence: textual, personal experience, etc.
5. Commentary
6. Theme
7. Call to action
8 Visuals.

In order to model deeper discussion, I took up class time to watch the videos and lead conversations, but as of late, I've flipped the classroom a bit and posted the videos on my classroom website and had them comment on particular aspects of the speech. Their comments, however, I find, are much better now than had I merely posted them with no classroom modeling first.

Once the students have an inkling of what might be expected of them at the end of the unit, they then form groups.

Collaboration and Differentiation Can Co-Exist

It all starts with creating collaborative groups that work independently on individual projects that, in the end, come together to create a group presentation. It's a method of differentiating while still keeping students accountable for their own work. Collaboration is a part of the Common Core Standards and assessments, but so are individual writing assignments, so we can't neglect either.

In terms of creating the groups, I allow student choice, but give them rules:

- There can only be four in a group (or whatever number you, the teacher, deem necessary for your project). I find four good because I can still control my goals to differentiate and I can successfully observe that number for accountability.

- The groups must be mixed gender. In a group of three boys, there must also be a girl. My rationale is this: depending on the girl, there's no way she will allow them to produce a weapon-driven theme. I've also seen the quieter girls, simply by their presence, reign in goofy boy behavior. Conversely, a group of three girls must also include a boy. I find this tends to temper certain management issues. I prefer not be witness to a quarter's worth of research on fashion's impact on dress code, and boys tend to sit naturally on the catty gene so prevalent with secondary girls.

- Kids who don't want to work in groups must do all the work themselves. Oh? You say you now want to collaborate and share the work? Great. Go find a group.

- I reserve the right to create groups, bust them apart, morph groups, etc. Sure, I'll give groups a reason, but they don't have to agree with it. This generally only happens after behind-the-scenes intervention or concerns have been brought to my attention.

OK, so the goals of the TED unit are for the groups to find a topic they can all research and become experts in. Each student will then communicate their group's findings in a different way. Thus, each student is responsible for a part of the whole project. If something doesn't get done, I'll know who dropped the ball. If all parts work together, the end result will be that much greater.

The end result is a combination of a written piece and a bigger project. The written piece is meant to inform the audience about the importance of the topic, the history of the topic, a possible problem that involves the concept, evidence to support the issue, and a solution that the students are pitching overall. The writing components break down as follows:

- Student #1—This student is in charge of writing the introduction complete with hook at the beginning of the writing and a thesis statement that is agreed upon by all members of the group. The thesis statement, after all, drives the order and content of the rest of the collaborative essay.
- Student #2—This student is in charge of writing a section on background information, setting up the reader/audience with reasons why this issue is important and where the information came from.
- Student #3—This student is in charge of writing a body section that includes evidence, data, an interview, and transition into the next body paragraph.
- Student #4—This student is in charge of writing a conclusion that includes a call to action or proposed solution to the issue at hand.

Notice, I don't call their contributions "paragraphs." That's because I want to encourage a relaxing on the traditional four to five paragraph scaffold. I would rather the students think in terms of "sections." These sections need to say what they need to say. There are no quantity limitations or expectations. Also, in terms of format, I think their informational writing needs to look closer to an executive summary than a typical essay. (See Chapter 5 on an executive summary format.) That is, the writing should be a combination of prose, bullets, lists, infographics, charts, explanations, and written commentary.

The visual projects are divided up between the students in the group. They choose who does what. The projects are as follows:

1. A website—We use Weebly to design a shell for a website that each group creates. A student is in charge of designing the shell for their group. Each student in the group gets his or her own page in which to display their writing and contributions, but it doesn't fall to the web designer to type it all in. The students must email their writing to their website designer to submit as is.

2. An infographic—Another student is in charge of designing an infographic to embed into the website. Infographics are all around us and are visual

representations of data and statistics. They use symbols, icons, images, numbers, charts, etc. There are a number of programs out there to help students create them digitally. Check out www.infogr.am or www.piktochart.com for some free options.

3. A PowerPoint, Prezi or Keynote (or another form of presentation software)—A student is also in charge of the visual flipchart that appears behind the speakers the day of their final presentation. If you look at TED speeches online, every one of them has a PowerPoint or something like that happening in the background of the oral presentation. This student must think about the order in which the group will be presenting, and must include both images and bulleted text to help illustrate what's being presented.

4. A news segment—Using key episodes of NPR's RadioLab as models, a student creates a three to five minute news segment that gets embedded into the website. This starts with writing a short script. Then, using GarageBand or Audacity or something like that, students can create a short news segment that must use a little music, spoken voice, and sound effects to get a point across to the listener. The topic simply must be related to the issue being researched. It can be a dramatized protest, an interview with an expert, an op-ed piece à la talk radio, etc.

Once responsibilities were chosen, from there groups created a collaboration constitution. This contract was a team charter that helped students create expectations for how to collaborate together. It also served as a rubric in which to assess each other at the end of the unit.

Following is the document that students used to help guide groups in creating their team charter.

Team Charter Template: Collaboration Constitution

You need to design a contract that all team members (and their parents/guardians) will sign. Think about the following as you draft your team charter:

1. What will be the roles and/or responsibilities of each member of the team as they relate to the project?

2. How often will you meet outside of school?

3. How will you communicate outside of school? (email, Skype, virtual classroom, phone, etc.?)

4. How much time passes before a reply to a question or comment is considered unacceptable?

5. What script can you develop or sentence stem can you use to tell someone they aren't holding their weight or participating the way they should?

6. What strategies can you develop in order to increase participation from members before coming to the teacher for intervention?

7. What are your deadlines?

8. What are the roles/responsibilities of each member as it relates to running the group? In other words, is there a group leader, recorder, timer, etc.?

9. What are the norms of your meetings?

10. Begin your collaboration constitution with a mission statement. A mission statement is an agreed upon set of goals that you all are setting out to accomplish. For instance:

> The mission of our group, Team _____, is to collaborate in order to develop the highest quality project we can present. We will abide by the rules of our constitution in order to research an issue, produce a website, and present our solutions together.

11. You will end your team charter with lines to be signed by all members of your team. Another copy of the document will go to each team member's home to be signed by a parent/guardian in order for him or her to understand the nature of the project in which you are participating.

Figures 3.1 and 3.2 show a couple of student samples from group constitutions.

Once groups have been made, jobs have been divvied up, and constitutions signed, the next step is in finding an advocacy topic on which all can agree.

For interdisciplinary subjects, if you decide to tackle a TED-esque unit, you might give them a short list of content-related topics from which to choose. That enables you to focus their research on your subject matter and still allow them to participate in this kind of rigorous project-based writing unit. For examples, see Table 3.1.

TABLE 3.1 Content-Related Topics for a Project-Based Learning Unit

Math	Science	History	Electives	PE
How do we straighten the Leaning Tower of Pisa?	How can we clean up the Pacific Ocean Trash Island?	Can the United States truly have a bi-partisan government?	Computers: What are the five most innovative up-and-coming technologies and how can we predict their impact?	How can we retain physical education programs in schools?
What will the population of the planet be in one hundred years?	How can we reverse global warming?	What will be the civil rights issues of the future?	Spanish: Can immigration law allow for a more global community?	Why is doping such a pervasive problem in professional sports?

TEAM CHARTER

The mission of our group, Team Pollution Police, is to collaborate in order to develop the highest quality project we can present. We will abide by the rules of our constitution in order to research an issue, produce a website, and present our solutions together.

good

Roles:

- **Infographic Creator (Aurealio Acosta)**
- **Visual Creator (Kaitlyn Lukjaniec)**
- **Website Creator (Josiephine Duong)**
- **Lead Speaker (Dennis Wong)**

Writing Responsibilities:

- **Introduction (Josiephine Duong)**
- **Background Info (Kaitlyn Lukjaniec)**
- **Evidence (Dennis Wong)**
- **Call to Action (Aurelio Acosta)**

Communication:

- **How- Right after school and on the weekends**
- **How Often- 1 or 2 times a week (Depending on what we need to do) for about an Hour.**
- **Where- At JMS and at team member's homes.**
- **Methods of dealing with people who are not working**
  1. **Talk to them about the problem.**
  2. **Email them and have them respond with what they were required to do with in 24 hour of the email.**
  3. **Have them come to a lunch project session and do what they need to complete.**

Norms:

1. **Must respond within 24 hours to any group work.**
2. **Be Attentive to All work.**
3. **Be on time/ No Procrastination**
4. **Attend all group meetings. Need a reason to be excused.**
5. **All have equal shares of work.**
6. **Don't get off topic.**
7. **Go beyond expectations.**
8. **No talking back when the group asks you to do something.**
9. **FOLLOW ALL NORMS AND RULES AS OUTLINED BY TEAM CHARTER!**

Kaitlyn | Aurelio | Josiephine

Kaitlyn | **Aurelio** | **Josiephine**

Dennis

Dennis Wong

FIGURE 3.1

Team Ace of Spades

Members: Allister, Desiree, Emily, Kathleen, Maverick

Roles: Allister – Group Leader, Radio Lab Director

Desiree – Visual and Website Leader

Emily – Visual Leader, Co-Leader

Kathleen – Website Leader

Maverick – Infographic Leader, Recorder

Communication: Meet once every other week on day everybody is open, Email 3 times per week of status report (Monday, Wednesday, and Friday at around 6:30)*

*must reply before next day

Norms:

1. Any arguments lead to a vote!
2. Majority wins the vote.
3. Pester the one who doesn't do their work by sending many emails or messages telling them to do their work.
4. If member still doesn't do work, contact parents.
5. If all else fails tell Mrs. Wolpert.
6. Email or alert other members if not able to come to meetings beforehand.
7. If fooling around or not listening, person will do pushups or will not get the reward.
8. Members will be rewarded if they have done all work with candy.
9. Everybody must participate and must be kind to each other even if they are enemies.*
10. Do not interrupt when someone talks.

*If a member is not participating, get them included and fighting is not tolerated.

Motto: "If we could ace a spade, then we could ace anything!"

Our commitment:

As Team Ace of Spades, we will do our best to get our work done in the highest quality, but also have fun at the same time. We do not want to get in trouble so we will follow all norms to make sure everything is in order. In conclusion, we will do our best, follow the rules, and have fun!

Sign Below:

Allister

Maverick   *Emily*

Desiree   *Kathleen*

FIGURE 3.2

Information Hunting: Breaking the Google Homepage Habit

The first thing to do in any class is to promote more rigorous and effective information hunting. Hunting is really what research is all about. It's about smelling a topic and following the leads until you find the facts that are your prey.

Some research is, obviously, going to be specific for each subject area. However, how we research, and the level of research that qualifies as acceptable, really needs to be a universal message. As each student enters each class, all subjects should be promoting similar expectations and techniques.

I'm not saying that every class has to carve out days in a row in the computer lab to teach research. I'm saying that the message must be consistent and teachers need to look for ways to assess that students are utilizing the tools of their generation.

When I am having the students do a research project, for example, I hone in on what I call "Breaking the Google Homepage Habit." I walk them through activities that focus on the following:

1. **Metasearching using Dogpile**—What I like about this is that on the page where your results are listed, it categorizes your results in ways that might behoove better research. If the student types in "global warming," then it asks if you would also like results that only focus on "causes of global warming," "effects of global warming," and so on.

2. **Google Advanced Search**—Obviously, the more specifically you search, the less work you have to do. Let Google do the work by spending just a little time creating parameters for your results.

3. **Google Scholar**—This can be a little heady, but it has also led to some really interesting results.

4. **Reading URLs**—What does .org mean? .gov? .edu? What symbols may indicate personal sites? Reading the sentences of the URL is the first step in reliable searching online.

5. **Follow the links**—where do the links go once you click on them? Do they go to a scholarly website or do they link to a T-shirt sale on CafePress?

6. **Triangulating the data**—Sure, you can start with something like Wikipedia. It's a jumping off place, after all. However, once you have a seemingly true fact, you need to then find three different sites other than Wikipedia that corroborate the information.

7. **Check the evidence**—Take a fact from a website. Say it's a date or name. Then Google only that. See what happens. It might lead you to more facts and evidence you can cite, or it might negate what you've found and make you question your initial lead.

To assess students on any of these skills, I then teach them how to take a screen shot (this means teaching them how to take one on both Mac and PC) to prove a particular step. For instance, I might ask them to use Google Advanced Search, enter their criteria, and have them turn in a screen shot of the Advanced Search page. They then turn this in for a homework assignment that counts as credit/no credit. If they turn it in, they have an opportunity for full points. If they don't, they get a 0. If they turn it in late, the 0 can get taken away for partial points. It's an easy skill they can prove they can do and an easy assignment to score.

By reiterating over and over throughout the year that I expect these steps to be utilized and followed, and by assessing them on occasion for them to prove the skills aren't getting dusty, it gets them started in more rigorous research with a little structure and guidance.

Then, as students begin to hone in on topics for their research projects, they begin to keep a running bibliography of the websites, articles, and multi-media presentations that may have been helpful while researching their topics. This bibliography serves as another score and can also be used for collaborative research between students and even classes.

Our initial research, however rigorous, was not the end of it. This just signaled a new step in agreeing on a topic in which to become experts.

Developing a Problem Statement Who

Once a certain amount of research has been done, we started full-force exploring possible topics about which to research, write, and speak. I told them that it was their choice to be excited by their topic because I wasn't assigning topics to them; they got to choose. Now, this option, while it can bring out the highest quality in the end product, can also shut some students down if not given some guidance. So to do that, I had *Junior Scholastic* magazines, newspapers, and printed-out articles strewn in duplicates on every table. In a timed activity, the students would grab a resource and skim for headlines and topics. After three minutes, they were told to switch resources, and so on. Additionally, we also had the classroom computers on the TED website where students could skim through the titles of the speeches to be inspired by the names, many of which are clues to the themes, problems, or solutions posed by the speaker.

Then we created five posters and stuck them up all over the room. These posters read: School Site, Local, State, National, and International, each representing the location or those most affected by the topic. We brainstormed lists for each of the posters, with students going up to the papers and writing a topic for all to see. In the end, we had a list of around 200 topics.

Nevertheless, just listing a topic like "Animal Abuse" is not enough to begin writing a great speech and it isn't enough to begin efficient research necessary to inform an audience.

We needed a problem statement. A problem statement is a paragraph that explains what they wish to write and speak about, and by following the paragraph outline, it also helps them narrow down their topic to something manageable, more specific, and ultimately easier to research. When we think about college and career readiness, a problem statement is used to prepare for a doctorate dissertation as well as with business proposals. So the trick for me was in scaffolding it down to the secondary level. In a sense what they did was write an abstract from the get-go rather than a summary after the fact.

Summary
their project

The end result was a guided worksheet that gave both an example and an outline for writing an informational problem statement. You can see the worksheet, courtesy of Teacher Created Resources, in Appendix D, or you can download it from www.routledge.com/eyeoneducation. The problem statement research paragraph can be broken down into four parts:

1. States the broad problem/topic about which you are interested in researching.
2. Defines the problem you will be solving by narrowing the issue.
3. Describes why it needs to be investigated by giving background information and context.
4. States the goals in writing and researching this problem (I will . . ., I plan . . ., I would like . . ., I propose . . ., etc.).

Then after writing the initial paragraph, they also developed three to five questions to help hone in on more specific future research should the group agree to focus on their topic. It's learning through inquiry, and in this case, it's decision-making through inquiry as well. The questions that students developed then became seeds for keywords that helped drive more efficient Google searching. See? It's all related.

Figures 3.3 through 3.5 show a few problem statements that were submitted, each of which focused on different content areas.

During the past few decades, the United States of America and its allies have been involved in several wars, in an attempt to make the world a safer place for all nations, but at what cost? Thousands of Americans have been killed during these wars, billions of dollars have been spent in the war effort, and not even most of the campaigns have been completely successful. For example, the Vietnam War was lost, the Korean War was a draw, and terrorist/extremist groups still wreak havoc in the Middle East. These wars have also unfortunately caused a large part of the world to hate the U.S. Furthermore, few of these wars were started because of a direct threat to the U.S., but mainly to other nations, some unaffiliated with U.S. These kinds of foreign wars also make for a huge delay in solving problems that are appearing in the U.S. itself. However, despite all this, it would be completely inhumane for the U.S. to ignore parts of the world where help is desperately needed, like in the Middle East. In the end, the United States needs to find a way to balance its role as policeman in the world with a way to solve problems that are happening on American soil.

Why is the U.S. constantly involved in wars in faraway countries?

How have the numerous wars fought affected the U.S. directly?

How could the U.S. try to maintain peace instead of declaring war?

What steps can be taken to stop American involvement in foreign wars?

How can the U.S. work with its allies to continue to fight necessary wars in foreign countries but still solve problems that have yet to be fixed in America itself?

FIGURE 3.3

Problem Statement: Nuclear Power 💣 = :BOOM:

      Nuclear power has always fascinated and terrified people for it's resourceful, but destructive powers. From generating our heat and electricity, to explosions and the widespread of radioactive materials into the air, nuclear power might just be an unaprehendable force that has no limitations, and knows no bounds. Many would say that the cons of nuclear power outweigh the pros; a darkside that calls sadness, sorrow, destruction, and the grim reaper to our world's stage. Death is just one of the many fears that comes within this atomic might. As a concerned student, I implore the united nations and the whole population of ~~their~~ people on this Earth to help eradicate. this destructive power, together.

Questions:

1.) How is nuclear power generated?

2.) How has the U.S gov't tried to stop other countries from developing nuclear power?

3.) What disasters have occured in response to atomic power?

4.) What is nuclear fission?

5.) What can the people do to eradicate nuclear power from ever existing?

FIGURE 3.4

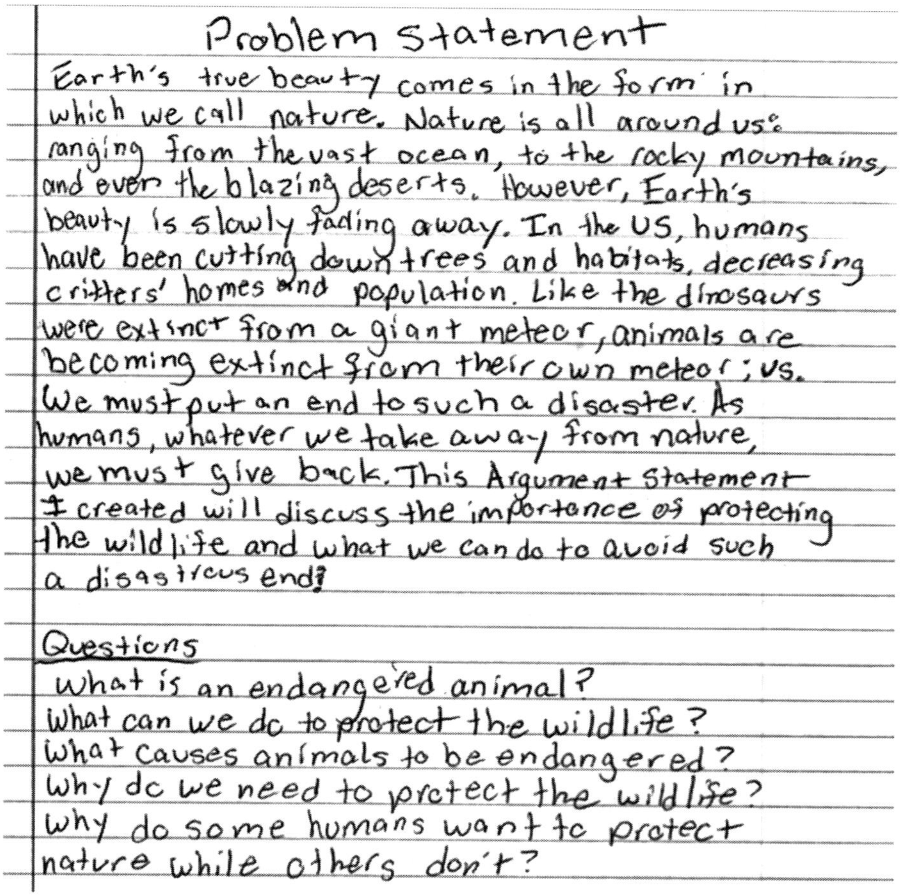

Problem Statement

Earth's true beauty comes in the form in which we call nature. Nature is all around us; ranging from the vast ocean, to the rocky mountains, and even the blazing deserts. However, Earth's beauty is slowly fading away. In the US, humans have been cutting down trees and habitats, decreasing critters' homes and population. Like the dinosaurs were extinct from a giant meteor, animals are becoming extinct from their own meteor; us. We must put an end to such a disaster. As humans, whatever we take away from nature, we must give back. This Argument Statement I created will discuss the importance of protecting the wildlife and what we can do to avoid such a disastrous end?

Questions
What is an endangered animal?
What can we do to protect the wildlife?
What causes animals to be endangered?
Why do we need to protect the wildlife?
Why do some humans want to protect nature while others don't?

FIGURE 3.5

By the way, students can even set up a news feed using those keywords to record articles and posts that mention the topic as they appear online. This digital briefcase of evidential writing and informational reading selections all starts with creating a formal problem statement.

The research each student and group produces can also be used in a collaborative way to help inform other students in other periods or classrooms in the school.

The Student-Created Resource Library

Remember, the Partnership of 21st Century Literacies states that the 4Cs should drive the method of how we teach the content and our expectations of what the students produce. That being said, I've developed a way for students to also collaborate across class periods in sharing their research and resources. Here's where the student-created resource library comes in.

Clearly, different students have different research challenges. Some have access to computers at home; some don't. Some have the moxie to problem solve; some have yet to develop this skill. Taking students to the computer lab often is tough. We simply don't have the time. But once we've done the initial research during class time to get the ball rolling, I then begin to ask them to research independently. For some, finding resources is hard without teacher guidance. But once they can submit a bibliographical log of the research they did in class, then that can become a tool for them to access when they are expected to research more independently. With the submission of the first wave of bibliographies based on class work, we now have artifacts of informational readings just waiting to be shared to help guide homework.

Once students honed in on their group topics, each student could then research a single list of ten resources that helped seed their informational writing. Therefore, in each period, I had my thirty-six students covering approximately nine topics, each with ten entries in their bibliographies. They each submitted a bibliography for a grade in the book that counted as a quiz. From there, they each inserted their bibliography into a manila folder that was labeled with their topic. These all went on the wall. As each period came in, those students with topics not represented on the wall filled out their own files and inserted their bibliographies, while those who saw their topics already posted inserted their bibliographies, adding to those provided by the students in first period. Therefore, we developed a wall of files of topics with websites and book titles that any student could access for further research.

By the end of the activity, those higher-level kids looking for additional resources had 'em. For those lower-level students still struggling to bring in a list of ten resources, they now had access to a vetted list of websites already available on their topics. These files became our interactive bulletin board for the whole unit, and all students had access to everyone's research.

Of course, there are also ways to do this same activity online using social bookmarks like CiteULike, Diigo, and Delicious. With resources stored online, students can share them with each other. A teacher can set up a classroom where students are able to view each other's bookmarks in much the same way as our file folders grant access to a certain level of transparent research.

Using social bookmarking sites is definitely a key skill for students to learn, but I find that while most students have access to computers these days (according to Pew Research 95 percent of all teens are online) that doesn't mean that they have access to collaboration tools. Also, as passionate as I am about educational technology, I do find that there are certain lessons we should be modeling still offline before taking it online. I think that by introducing my students to the concept of a student-created resource library in the classroom first, I will more likely be able to translate the intent of social bookmarking later in the school year. Besides, now I don't have to hear an excuse about not having found any research due to lack of connectivity. And ensuring that all students have the tools to participate is as important as exposing all students to the tools of their future.

The Importance of Visualizing Data

The importance of creating charts and graphs has always been relegated to the maths and sciences. But with the advent of infographics, we have a more artistic way to present data. In a way, an infographic is more real world because it's a small multi-genre project (see Chapter 6) in itself. It is a blending of the arts and sciences that visualize data.

It seems like everywhere you look these days you see infographics. You see them in every newspaper, in magazines, in websites, in brochures. They incorporate multiple elements of informational writing in the form of symbols, icons, images, pictures, text, bullets, charts, graphs, etc. They can tap into a macro issue, but still be made up of micro pieces of information.

I asked my students to create infographics based on their advocacy issues. Of course, a student can develop an infographic based on any subject.

- In Spanish class, a student can create an infographic based on Mexican tourism.
- In PE, a student can create an infographic based on a sport's history.
- In science, a student can create an infographic based on the discovery and use of an element.
- In math, a student can create an infographic based on seasonal spending facts.
- In history, a student can create an infographic based on the casualties comparing different wars.

The first step in expecting a student to produce an infographic is, of course, to introduce them to recognizing them. Post a few for the class and begin a whole class discussion on the symbols that are used, the overall topic, and the multiple pieces of evidence a single infographic can provide.

From there, simply ask students to turn in an example of a real infographic that they can find out there in the real world. This can prove to be a simple assignment for them to produce and an equally easy one to score. Again, it's a credit/no credit assignment. Their infographic can be one torn from a magazine or printed from a website. Use these stacks that come in as seeds for same-day discussions that are driven by the students themselves.

The subsequent discussions help fuel the next step, which is to have the students read and analyze them independently. For instance, I have given my students the following assignment:

Look at the following infographic from Princeton University:

http://www.princeton.edu/~ina/infographics/water.html

Examine it closely, and then analyze the infographic in two to four paragraphs. Remember to cite the graphic specifically as evidence for your analysis. Each of the following questions does not need to be in its own paragraph. Instead, find a way to organize your thoughts so that your short-answer essay includes all of the necessary responses.

1. Based on what you know about the components of the word, what does the word "infographic" mean?

2. What is the overarching issue that the infographic describes?

3. An infographic is like an essay, but it uses symbols, images, text, and data to prove and persuade. It is rich with information. What was the most stunning or interesting piece of information that you learned from this graphic?

4. What symbols were used to create this infographic? (Feel free to bullet your responses.)

5. Looking at text structure, how does the artist highlight a particular topic or draw your attention to a particular element?

6. Who are the sources of this information?

By asking all students to recognize, read, and analyze infographics, you are preparing the students to one day create their own. Some of those students are already doing so for the TED unit. Others might choose to design an infographic as a project for a class in which they must report on informational data. This way, they are set to help others visualize the data in way that honors the 4Cs, real-world applications, and 21st century learning.

Figures 3.6 and 3.7 show student infographic examples. They were created using one of two websites:

■ Infogr.am (That's no typo; that's the real website.)

■ Piktochart.com.

FIGURE 3.6

California's Budget

education **is** the most powerful weapon
-Nelson Madela

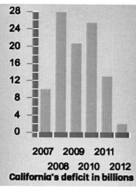

2007 2009 2011
2008 2010 2012
California's deficit in billions

If your school had to make cuts, what should they cut first?
Question asked by L.A. Youth for survey.

1. School Newspaper/Broadcast Outlet
2. Summer School
3. Field Trips
4. Security Guards
5. Custodians
6. Libraries
7. Art and Music
8. Sports
9. Guidance Counselors
10. Other
11. Administrators
12. Teachers

Education is not preparation for life;
education is life itself.
-John Dewey

Impact of Budget Cuts on Community Colleges

According to a survey taken by California Community Colleges system, an estimated 20% of students who attended community college had to be placed on a wait list for classes last fall because the colleges have had more than 809 million dollars cut from their budget in the last three years. The total enrollment have dropped by 510,000 students from the peak year of 2008-2009 when there were about 3,000,000 students. One contributing factor to the diminishing student enrollment is the price of the enrollment fees. Enrollment fee have increased by 200%, from 26$ in 2010 to 46$ today.

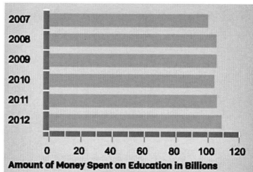

Amount of Money Spent on Education in Billions

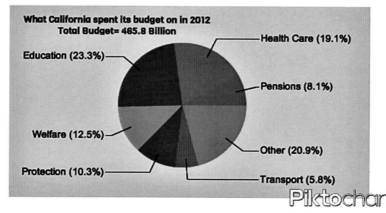

What California spent its budget on in 2012
Total Budget= 465.8 Billion

Education (23.3%)
Health Care (19.1%)
Pensions (8.1%)
Welfare (12.5%)
Other (20.9%)
Protection (10.3%)
Transport (5.8%)

Piktochart

FIGURE 3.7

Another option in visualizing data is in using data motion charts. A motion chart takes lists of data and animates them so you can see the visual of the data change over time. Hans Rosling, arguably one of the most entertaining statisticians in the world, has cultivated this merging of visual and statistics for his Gapminder website (www.gapminder.org). They take world data, like the stats found on such sites as the World Health Organization, and convert them to a moving graphic. His site is full of wonderful examples that students can cull for their own research.

A great and engaging example for this technology is included in his TED speech, "Stats that Reshape Your World View." You can also see a short example that is perfect to show secondary students from a segment produced by the BBC called "200 Countries, 200 Years, 4 Minutes—The Joy of Stats."

However, if students want to animate their own findings of statistics and data, they need not look far. Google acquired Gapminder's technology and can, through its motion charts program, create a simpler yet effective animated effect. It's one of many ways one can showcase their research.

Uncommon Assessments to Show Informational Research (Even in a Narrative Unit)

In my narrative chapter of this book (Chapter 4), I explore both how inter-disciplinary subjects can inject narrative strategies and how language arts teachers can inject more nonfiction techniques. One of the activities I had students create required them, while writing science fiction or historical fiction short stories, to focus on their researched facts rather than their created fictional plot points. Though the students wrote short stories, the fact is that we focused as much on the accuracy of the history and science as we did on the story structure itself. As such, I found ways students proved the informational research that they embedded into their narratives. These became their own assignments and assessments leading up to the final essay submissions.

A content-area teacher can use these similar assignments to have students showcase their own informational research regardless of the content. In the following sections, I am going to introduce four activities and/or skills to showcase informational research.

Independent Bibliographical Format Checks

There were two research checks that I conducted over the course of the unit. For these, the students needed to follow proper APA format and produce a bibliography of at least ten resources to prove they were researching informational texts to seed their narratives with facts. I provided a link on the assignments checklist for students to refer to as they worked on their bibliographies. Even though I worked with them on basic APA format, nobody is an expert in every kind of resource. Providing a link for them to use on their own time helped shape their own independent learning. The link I provided was this one: http://owl.english.purdue.edu/owl/resource/560/01/

Google Search Story

Another way the students showed me their informational research was to produce a Google Search Story. Never seen one? They are so cool! Here are some examples:

- "Brother and Sister" www.youtube.com/watch?v=Fy5LGfZgv04
- "Harry Potter" www.youtube.com/watch?v=AbprAKGAg8U

Apparently, Google produced them as commercials, but so many people wanted to know how to make them that they made a "video creator." Don't get excited, however. Google deleted the video creator recently and teachers are mourning the loss of a great educative tool. Nevertheless, it was a cool enough activity that I wanted to describe it here because I think that there was and continues to be great value in combining visuals with informational research.

Before Google deleted the all-time coolest tool around, the students had to take the key URLs that helped to guide their research and order them in such a way as to create their own narratives. It's informational writing and research structured in such a way as to promote storytelling. A science, history, math, or electives teacher, however, could have them produce Google Search Stories without a narrative structure, but that combined facts with music. The music that the students choose helps to set the tone of the overall project.

What if . . .

From there, as a final *pièce de resistance*, the students had to produce a "What if . . ." presentation that incorporated both writing and images. Larry Ferlazzo, a magnificent award-winning teacher from Sacramento, CA, first turned me on to these projects. Basically, the students look at the historical era in which their book or story is set or the scientific principles on which the book or stories focus, and they figure on an alternative universe in which something factual did not exist.

For example, let's say a student is reading *The Hunger Games*. There is a lot of science in there, particularly science that focuses on spy technology and weaponry. The student researches real technology that exists now and then deletes one invention from our own timeline. They then imagine the ripple effect that this would cause.

First, the students analyzed a real "What if . . ." In this case, a long-lost speech of President Nixon's that he was prepared to deliver in the event the first astronauts had died during their famous trip. You can find the speech here: www.archives. gov/press/press-kits/american-originals-photos/moon-disaster-1.jpg. The students then needed to answer the following prompt:

Prompt: "That's one small step for man; one giant leap for mankind." The late, great Neil Armstrong was the first man to walk on the moon. He used beautiful language to immortalize this moment when he spoke these words. But what if this moment hadn't happened? What if the astronauts had died in their attempt to make history? It turns out President Nixon had been prepared for such a moment.

Using our expository paragraph format and textual evidence, analyze this "What if . . ." speech. It captures a moment in history that never was, but one we were prepared for.

(To learn more about possible expository paragraph formats, check out Chapter 2.)

From there, the students created a three to five slide PowerPoint that followed the ripple of changes in their "What if . . ." imaginings.

Hyperlinking

One other way the students show me their research is in providing at least ten hyperlinks throughout their essays, regardless of whether they are writing short stories or argumentation essays. Linking is, in my view, a vital skill for a young writer to know how to do. I think that all students should leave middle school knowing how to show an additional layer of information in all of their writings. These links allow a reader to confirm an author's research in a way that a simple bibliography list does not. It also allows a relationship between the student author and the reader in that a link indicates to the audience information that might prove interesting for further reading. Linking takes reading from a 2D experience to a 3D one. It also potentially adds a different modality to the essay by linking to images, webpages, or videos. It takes reading a student narrative from a static experience to a dynamic one.

In the end of my informational/narrative unit, the students needed to produce a story that focused on historical fiction or science fiction. They proved their informational research using a Google Search Story, and a "What if . . ." presentation. It was a narrative plus informational reading and writing unit that infused history and science into the ELA classroom.

The students became experts in either historical or scientific facts. Notice, I did not become the expert in those facts. I'm not a history or science teacher. What I am, however, is a writing guide. I guided them in how to communicate and maneuver through their subjects. The writing that I guided them towards became a vessel that delivered the material. In so doing, I was able to maintain teaching narrative and all the rich yummy writing elements that go along with it, and still address the informational requirements of the Common Core Standards.

As a language arts teacher, it can be hard to let go of some of the narrative teachings that we love, but one clearly does not have to. In fact, I would even go so far as to say that there is even a place for teaching narrative strategies in any content-area classroom.

Interested in other resources to help guide your content-area informational writing? Check out the following resources:

- *Content-Area Writing: Every Teacher's Guide* by Harvey Daniels, Steven Zemelman, and Nancy Steineke.
- *Teacher's Essential Guide Series: Content Area Writing* by Jim Burke.
- *Content Area Reading and Writing: Fostering Literacies in Middle and High School Cultures* (2nd edition) by Norman Unrau.
- *Coaching Writing in Content Areas: Write-for-Insight Strategies, Grades 6–12* (2nd edition) by William J. Strong.

4

Narrative

There's a Place for it in All Disciplines

Write narratives to develop real or imagined experiences or events using effective technique, relevant descriptive details, and well-structured event sequences.

(Common Core Standards)

I wanted to take a moment here to discuss narrative strategies. There is a myth that because narrative appears as a smaller percentage in secondary writing classes, perhaps the ability to use its techniques is less important in the eyes of Common Core. This is false.

In fact, without narrative techniques, your argument would be nothing more than a summary plus an opinion. The argument itself would not be convincing without narrative strategies on your side. Your informational writing assignments would come in as dry as a desert, the passion for the subject dissipated, leaving behind mere regurgitation of fact.

Narrative writing belongs, to a certain degree, in every classroom. It is, to many students, the "fun" writing genre. ELA teachers get to see this. However, if we can weave narrative techniques into other categories of writing, then that fun aspect begins to bleed and ripple into other units as well. Narrative strategies infuse your content with creativity and that added layer of student personality aids in ownership of the content.

So I wanted to share some lessons and expectations that could be used without sacrificing content time. In fact, I believe that once you incorporate some narrative techniques into your own modeled writing and into the assignments they are expected to produce, they will be more engaged in your topic and you will be more engaged in reading what they have created.

The Infusion of Narrative Elements into Interdisciplinary Content

Even though narrative writing doesn't hold as much weight in the eyes of the Common Core Standards, it is undoubtedly valuable in luring students to learning. Regardless of the subject matter, every class can ask students about themselves as they relate to their content, and every class should. Every class can ask for vivid descriptions. Every class can ask for writings that include sequence, plot, and message.

For instance, at the beginning of each year, I ask my students the following journal prompts:

- Your history as a reader
- Your history as a writer.

I ask them to fill out a reading survey about their likes, dislikes, what genre they pick up the most, whether they choose to read at all. It is a form of narrative writing in that they are answering questions about themselves in regards to literacy.

As a reluctant math student in my earlier years, I often wish I had been permitted to write about my relationship with the topic. I think my teacher would have seen that my interest in geometry could be tapped to help what I felt to be the more intimidating subject of algebra. Perhaps my frustrations could have been addressed earlier by simply asking me my own history as a mathematician.

Additionally, perhaps my science teachers would have recognized more in me than just a student who was confused by the maths and sciences. After all, while math freaked me out, I loved, and I mean loved, science. In fact, in second grade, when I was student of the week in Mrs. Douglas' class at Wonderland Ave. School, my poster read:

This is Heather. She likes science.

It was the first time I remember reading the word. After all, I brought in bugs every week in jars, so my teacher made it a part of my narrative that other kids knew about me. My interest in science became a proud part of my life story. In high school, even while I was getting a C in math, I took advanced biology, honors biology, and AP bio just because I enjoyed the subjects, not because I did particularly well in them. To this day, I thank Mr. Porter for allowing me to take those advanced science classes, not because I excelled in the fundamental science classes, but because I was so curious and persistent about understanding more advanced scientific concepts. I remember dissecting and discussing. I remember getting into an argument with this numbskull of a chemistry teacher, Mr. Allen, who despite being a gorgeous surfer was a dimwit of a teacher. I couldn't understand, for instance, why:

1 mole + 1 mole = 1 mole

What?! That goes against all reasoning. I kept asking to please have that explained again. In response, Mr. Allen said, "Heather, you don't have the understand it; just memorize the equation. You keep asking so many questions. You stand out in a crowd."

Naturally, I replied, "The thing about you, Mr. Allen, is that you care that you stand out in a crowd." It was my first time I can remember getting red-faced mad with a teacher, and it was all about science. See? I may be an ELA teacher now, but I have a relationship to share about science. Narrative in action.

Narrative is, in my view, the easiest genre to teach because students come in with a lot of the background knowledge they need to succeed at it. They come in with personal experiences to tap into. They come in with opinions and observations to relate.

There are a few key lessons with narrative writing that all teachers should be able to recognize when asking students to bring themselves to the table. These few components are not the end-all, be-all of the genre, but if a teacher of any subject has an understanding of each of these elements, then they can praise a student when they see them or ask a student to use them in any of their content-area writing. To prioritize, I believe there is a list of narrative concepts that teachers in areas outside of ELA ought to be aware of. They are as follows:

- Figurative language
- Sequence (plot structure)
- Theme.

I want to go into a little more detail of each of these components, but know that these are not elements I believe math and science and history teachers should be responsible to teach, but rather, they could be responsible to praise, assess, and expect. In so doing, they will be supporting the ELA teachers and the job that they must do. They will also be pulling a better quality of work and comprehension out of their students as well.

Figurative language communicates ideas over and beyond literal meaning of the initial words. We're talking about metaphors and similes. We're talking about hyperbole and sensory details. When asking students to write, using figurative language brings in a method of using comparisons from outside the realm of the definitions of the words in order to highlight their meaning. Imagine using hyperbole to describe the destruction from a volcano. Imagine using sensory details to draw a comparison between an equation in the textbook and where it appears in the world beyond school. While a teacher doesn't have to require the use of figurative language, it might be important to note that a student who utilizes this strategy might illustrate a real deep comprehension of material. Figure 4.1 is an excerpt from a student's science writer's notebook. In it, she uses narrative techniques to describe the cow's eye she has recently dissected. I've annotated some of the techniques.

Sequencing is a term used in many disciplines, but in writing it's about telling a story in chronological order. If we were talking about informational writing (see Chapter 3) we would also be discussing how information could be described in a step-by-step manner, which is how this multi-genre blending occurs. In narrative writing, however, we are talking plot structure and a student's ability to write a beginning of a tale, something that introduces the characters and the conflict/problem; the middle of the story with a ramping up towards the problem—is there a turning point, is there a realization of some kind?—and the end where all is resolved. Plot structure is vital in writing stories, but it can be used in other classes as well.

Look at the storyboards in Figures 4.2 and 4.3. These are examples of a project that some students produced to show the sequence of the historical fiction poem,

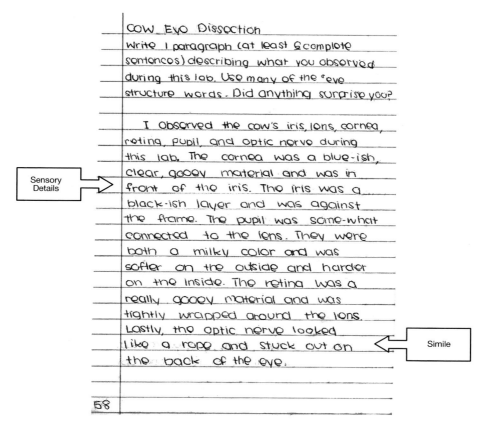

Cow Eye Dissection
Write 1 paragraph (at least 6 complete sentences) describing what you observed during this lab. Use many of the "eye structure words. Did anything surprise you?

   I observed the cow's iris, lens, cornea, retina, pupil, and optic nerve during this lab. The cornea was a blue-ish, clear, gooey material and was in front of the iris. The iris was a black-ish layer and was against the frame. The pupil was some-what connected to the lens. They were both a milky color and was softer on the outside and harder on the inside. The retina was a really gooey material and was tightly wrapped around the lens. Lastly, the optic nerve looked like a rope and stuck out on the back of the eye.

58

Sensory Details

Simile

FIGURE 4.1

"Paul Revere's Ride." You'll notice that they incorporated not only visuals but textual evidence as well.

Now, just imagine using this type of sequencing technique to show the steps of an equation towards its solution. It's an uncommon assessment using both visuals and writing. And the chunked writing can then be used as a rough draft to a more formal, final writing assessment. Case in point, Figure 4.4 is an example of a math storyboard. And Figure 4.5 is the follow-up of an analysis based on the brief explanations used in the project.

Theme is a universal expectation for teachers to assign and assess. Acknowledging the theme of a story or a selection or a biography or a discovery is a real tip-of-the-hat to an awareness of the overall message in life. A science teacher can ask what is the message, or overall impact, of a particular principle. A history teacher can ask what is the moral that we can all learn from reflecting on a particular era. Seeing the theme, the overall message, which can be derived from a lesson, is a skill that every teacher can encourage and develops an awareness of the macro-lesson in every teaching.

FIGURE 4.2

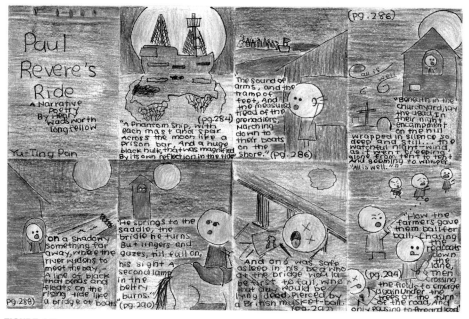

FIGURE 4.3

FIGURE 4.4

You can solve an equation and find the unknown "**x**" value by isolating the **x**, or variable. For example, if you had a problem like "3x+2=11". You can't solve for the equation and multiply **x** by 3, because you don't know the value of **x** is, and that's what we're going to find out. We will become detectives by finding out what the mysterious **x** is. First, we have to isolate the **x** by getting rid of the 3 and 2 on the same side of the equation. Let's get rid of that pesky 2 that is keeping us from **x**'s secrets. To get rid of 2, we want to "cancel it out" by subtracting 2 from 2 (to equal zero). If we do something to one side of the equation, we have to do it to the other side so, 11 is now 11-2, which is 9. What's left is 3x= 9. Now 3 is a really sticky guy, to get rid of him, we have to divide because 3÷3=1 and 1 multiplied by **x**= **x**. From there, we can find out the value of **x**. But in order to divide 3 from 3x, you have to divide 3 from both sides of the equation in order for the equation to be equal. Once you divide both sides by 3, you will get the final answer, x=3. So, to isolate the variable, you need to subtract and divide to reach the desired value of **x**!

FIGURE 4.5

Incorporating Informational Writing into a Narrative Unit

OK, so I devoted a section of this book to introducing non-ELA content areas to the glory of teaching narrative. But there's another reason why I've decided to devote a section of this book to narrative: the growls in every ELA department meeting regarding the Common Core that centers around a reluctance to part with the genre that they love to teach. See, incorporating informational writing and reading into one's content cannot be left to the STEM and history and electives alone. ELA must get on board as well.

As language arts teachers, we can no longer leave factual writing to those other subjects and solely teach the beauty and lyricism of writing during our narrative unit. Nope. We have to find a way to blend the two. A myth about the Common Core expectations upon us is that somehow we need to ditch narrative. That's false. The fact is that what we need to do is fold in informational, factual writing while still encouraging beautiful writing. One way to do this is in tweaking what we stress in our story-writing units.

According to the Common Core, while other subject areas are now expected to utilize writing, ELA is now expected to utilize other content areas. In the spirit of that latter goal, I wanted to share my first quarter unit. My department still wanted to teach narrative, but we also acknowledged that we needed more informational reading and writing to address the Common Core Standards. So I got to work with my mental wrench, tweaking and revising my narrative quarter, and what resulted in this unit is a magic combination of the two. It looks complex from the start, but it ended up being a rigorous and integrated unit that was far richer than my narrative unit of old.

My narrative unit now focuses on historical fiction and science fiction writing. It's a unit that uses strategies and assessments that can be tapped into for many informational reading and writing units, but I wanted to house these activities in a narrative shell so that other ELA teachers could see that lyrical writing is not a dead and lost art form in a common core world.

First off, I developed a checklist of assignments. To see the checklist of assignments I initially give to my students at the top of the unit, see Appendix E at the back of this book.

So, for the benefit of ELA teachers out there who are worried about what it might take to infuse their narrative unit with informational and interdisciplinary facts, I am going to go through the key assignments for the unit to describe them each as individual assessments and how they relate to each other as a whole. The unit itself is a huge smorgasbord of Common Core integrated goodness. The overall goal of the narrative unit was to do one of two things:

- Create a fan fiction short story based on a book of the student's choice. Fan fiction is a new genre of sorts that allows a reader to continue experiencing a beloved literary universe. Loved *The Hunger Games*? How about writing it from Prim's point of view or thinking about what would have happened if Gale had been selected instead of Peeta?

- Students could instead create a short story à la R.A. Montgomery's *Choose Your Own Adventure* series. Remember those? In those books, you start off with exposition that introduces you to the characters, setting, and conflict. From there, the reader has choices that take them, in a non-linear way, through the story. If you want to enter the UFO turn to page such and such. If you want to run away, turn to page so and so.

Here's the first targeted Common Core informational tweak I made to the unit: the books from which the students could choose to base their stories on had to be either historical fiction or science fiction. Therefore, we could then study the facts embedded into the fiction and seed researched information into the stories we wrote ourselves.

You can see the overall unit in Appendix E of this book, but I will break down key assignments in the following sequential list.

1. To begin to seed excitement over the unit, I began by guiding small groups to create inquiry charts. An inquiry chart uses a graphic organizer (like a web, Venn diagram, dual-entry journal, etc.) to explore different topics. In our charts, the students explored the similarities and differences between science or history and the fictionalized versions of these subjects. Since I gave students a choice between reading one of the two genres, I needed to first guide them to make an educated decision in which to read. First, we examined what literary elements went into both reading genres. The students created posters that were divided as follows: science vs. science fiction and history vs. historic fiction. Some students chose to focus on comparing the two: science fiction vs. historic fiction.

2. I then gave students time to select their books, after which they brought them in to share.

3. I grouped the students by reading genres, creating new table groups formed by those interested in one genre or the other. This made for interesting groups of students, selected not by level but on interest. There were still differences, however. Some groups had students whose books focused on different eras. At one table might be a student reading *Sherlock Holmes* (a higher-level book) as well as one reading *Dragonwings* (grade-level) or even *By The Great Hornspoon* (lower-level book). At another table might be a student reading *The Hunger Games* while another student read *Ender's Game*. Cool mix of both history and science in an ELA classroom.

4. The ultimate goal was to produce a fan fiction or *Choose Your Own Adventure*, but this first began with becoming familiar with the genres. One assignment I did asked students to analyze other pieces of fan fiction. Sure, I could ask students to just explore www.fanfiction.net; however, a lot of fan fiction out there stinks and is also questionably appropriate, so I pulled some decent examples produced by my students from previous years and shared them with my current classes. Here are a few for you to check out:
   - *Zeus*—a fan fiction narrative based on Percy Jackson https://dl.dropbox.com/u/4234943/zeus.docx
   - *Prim's Perspective*—a fan fiction based on *The Hunger Games* https://dl.dropbox.com/u/4234943/Prim%27s%20Perspective.docx
   - *No Heroes Allowed*—a fan fiction based on Harry Potter https://dl.dropbox.com/u/4234943/Fanfiction_20Ron_20Weasley-1.rtf
   - *The Tribute from District 2*—a fan fiction based on *The Hunger Games* https://dl.dropbox.com/u/4234943/Tribute%20from%20District%2012.doc
   - *Three to Two*—a fan fiction based on Harry Potter https://dl.dropbox.com/u/4234943/Three%20to%20Two%20fan%20fiction.docx.

The current students then had to analyze one of the pieces of fan fiction and answer the following prompt. This counted as a homework assignment.

Prompt: You are writing and posting a formal multiple-paragraph literary analysis that gives your opinion of the short piece of fan fiction you selected. Evaluate the fan fiction narrative of your choice, giving your opinion of the story. You do not need to have read the source material in order to appreciate the stories. You may use your prior knowledge, your Pixar Rules, and any research you wish as evidence of your expertise. Think about the elements of narratives, and make sure you evaluate the story using your narrative know-how. Show off what you know about what goes into a great narrative.

5. I showed students a great narrative resource: Pixar's 22 Rules of Storytelling. Then, they produced an analysis of their favorite rule. This poster is an infographic of shorts that combines both text with a picture, and it's rich with informational how-to set to the tune of narrative advice. This analysis went hand in hand with the fan fiction assignment. You can find the poster here: http://i.imgur.com/DH1lF.jpg. We looked at each rule as a whole class and, after small group discussion, the students then had to answer the following prompt:

Prompt: Construct a formal analysis based on the poster listing Pixar's 22 Rules of Storytelling. Your analysis needs to be a multiple paragraph essay that includes, but is not limited to, the following information:

- Use evidence from the rules to tell me what you find could have the most significant impact on your writing.
- Describe a book you have read or a movie you have seen that incorporates a number of examples from these rules.
- Describe a book you have read or a movie you have seen that has broken these rules, and is, thus, a bad example of storytelling.
- Describe a book you have read or a movie you have seen that has broken these rules, yet nevertheless is a great story. After all, there are no hard and fast rules in storytelling.

6. From there, we went into the computer lab and worked a bit on some Internet literacy and reliable safe searching (see Chapter 8) in order to conduct the research necessary to inject fact into their original historic fiction or science fiction narratives.

7. The students then produced written and technology-influenced projects that served as assessments for their informational research. They had to do the following:

- Provide at least ten hyperlinks throughout their story that linked to factual evidence of their research.
- Create a Google Search Story that highlighted key URLs that aided in their research. These URLs had to be organized to show a story arch.
- Develop a bibliography using proper APA format.
- Present a "What if . . ." oral presentation that mused about what would happen if one of the facts infused in their narratives (either a scientific fact or a historical one) had not occurred.

See, it's a myth that the Common Core Standards have done away with narrative altogether. Actually, the only twist is that we need to be highlighting argument and informational writing more. But by blending the two and teaching narrative in a more multi-genre format, we can kill two birds with one stone. (See Chapter 6 for more on the multi-genre format.)

Ready to try your hand at teaching more narrative strategies? Check out these resources for further information:

- *Narrative Writing: Learning a New Model for Teaching* by George Hillocks, Jr.
- *Storycraft: The Complete Guide to Writing Narrative Nonfiction* (Chicago Guides to Writing, Editing, and Publishing) by Jack Hart.

5

1-20-'16

Summary: Get to the Point!

nothing really new

The Underrated Writing Genre

> Whether you are writing for the workplace or for academic purposes, you will need to research and incorporate the writing of others into your own texts. Two unavoidable steps in that process are paraphrasing (changing the language into your own) and summarizing (getting rid of smaller details and leaving only the primary points).
>
> (Purdue OWL (Online Writing Lab))

The ability to summarize is often taken for granted. To us, it seems like a simple concept: get to the main idea, the heart of the matter, the gist. Yet summarization is actually a 21st century skill as listed by the Partnership of 21st Century Literacies.

I mean, think about it. You summarize an issue when writing an email. You summarize conversations. You summarize units and chapters. It's unavoidable, but it isn't something we all naturally do well. So we must teach students how to summarize at the level that we want.

We take summarization for granted, but it's a hard skill to achieve. You wouldn't think so, but summarization is difficult for many students and for many reasons. For secondary students, I think the difficulty lies in part because it's such a "me-centric" stage. "Why get to the point, when I like to hear myself speak?" I also think there's a bit of the myth going on in their heads of more equals more. "If I say more, then eventually I'll hit on it." But it ends up sometimes like trying to hit a target the size of a pea with a boulder. You might hit it, but you also might not see the pea when you're through with the pitch. When I teach summarization, I tell students the following:

> Summary is about precision. It is about finding the needle in the haystack. It is about only the most important points, and not the ones you can live without. And while you're at it: the summary gods do not care about your opinion. In fact, they will smite you if you inject voice or judgment into your summary. Summary is all about paraphrasing what you read, not inferring what is not in your face. Bottom line: summary can be boring.

OK, before you get all mad that I called a writing genre boring, that fact is that with secondary students, they are like horses ready for the race to start. They stand behind the gate, clipping at the ground, eager to give their opinions and challenges.

But that's not summary's purpose. Instead, it's all about paraphrasing someone else's writing.

Sometimes, to a secondary student, writing genres are really categorized into two categories: interesting and boring. Summary generally falls into the latter.

As a result, the quality of writing that ends up being produced can read too simple, not representing the rigor of the actual skill. Because it seems simple, we tend to get simplistic versions of summary. When, in fact, it can be challenging to write a great summary; and along with argumentation, summary is also a universal writing genre that spans across all content areas.

For this reason, it has to be taught in a targeted way. Below, I have included a few activities and strategies to teach summary or, at least, to indicate your expectation of summary. Each activity can be done using the content in the classroom.

One of the keys in teaching summary is in asking for it consistently. I'm not saying that just because you continuously assign it, it will magically begin to happen, but if you vary the assignments, both formal and informal, the students will eventually get the message. In the activities and assignments below, you will notice that each one tackles summary in a different way. Some ask for full paragraphs; others merely ask for sentences. These are all building blocks for a deceptively difficult skill that is important for any student in any classroom.

The Summary Card

The summary card is a quick way to use summarizing in the classroom. This card (Figure 5.1) is one that is an informal, summative assessment of a student's reading. I'm not a big believer in reading logs, but something like a summary card might still give a teacher evidence of what a student has read and what he or she understands. In this case, the following summary card is used in an ELA classroom. It is meant to be submitted after a student has read an independent reading book. These cards then go onto a ring that hangs in the classroom library so that other students can read a little about the book to decide if it might be their next selection. It's a way for peers to advise peers.

Now, the key here is to take what ELA has developed and incorporate this into your own content. Perhaps summary cards can be designed and implemented for the ends of chapters or units. Perhaps students can submit cards that reflect the chapters of textbooks that most engaged them. It's a way to summarize information in a quick assessment of both content and writing quality.

Chunking Text

Chunking text is a way to teach not only summary writing but also informational reading and literacy. It's a trick that allows students to tackle only one section of reading at a time.

A teacher may take an article, for instance, and break it down into parts so that students are only required to paraphrase a small chunk at a time. These short paraphrases then get pushed together using transitional words, phrases, and

```
┌─────────────────────────────────────────────────────────────────────────┐
│  Title                                              Your Name             │
│  Author                                             Recommend?  ☐    ☐    │
│  Genre                                                          Y    N    │
│                                                                           │
│  Summary: A summary is a 1–2 paragraph description of a book/story that   │
│  gives NO OPINION. It only states the facts. It is in your own words      │
│  unless a direct quote is used. In that case, remember to use quotation   │
│  marks. Basic rules to follow in a summary:                               │
│                                                                           │
│           I. Main Topic Sentence                                          │
│                A. Include a Title, Author, Genre (TAG)                    │
│                B. Keep this next sentence general                         │
│          II. Remember to . . .                                            │
│                A. Only use the most important points                      │
│                B. Disregard little details                                │
│                C. Use transitions                                         │
│                D. Go in chronological order                               │
│                E. Don't use voice                                         │
│                F. Use sentence variety                                    │
│                G. NO SPOILERS!                                            │
│         III. Conclusion                                                   │
│                A. Don't give your opinion!                                │
│                                                                           │
│  Remember, it is NOT a literary analysis. DO NOT ANALYZE OR RESPOND TO    │
│  THE LITERATURE. The skill you are being tested on is whether or not you  │
│  can recognize the main idea and most important details. Period.          │
│                                                                           │
└─────────────────────────────────────────────────────────────────────────┘
```

FIGURE 5.1

punctuation (see Chapter 7 for a list of transitional techniques) in order to smooth out the writing quality.

As an example, take a look at the math-related article in Figure 5.2. Notice that it has lines that indicate sections a teacher wants the student to chunk.

Figure 5.3 is the final result of the activity, including transitional words and phrases.

What's the Big Idea?

"What's the big idea?" is an exercise developed by a wonderful ELA teacher, Elizabeth Harrington, a Writing Project Fellow and accomplished teacher leader. This activity really gets students to the point of a reading selection. It asks students to read a short piece from any content area and pull out the main idea in their own words. It's a great opening activity or short, informal written assignment.

Take a piece from some kind of informational writing and then ask students to summarize the main idea. Figure 5.4 gives a few examples.

These single statements can then be flushed out to become full summaries or can serve as their own submission to assess students on their ability to identify the most important points of their content.

Cornell Notes

Cornell Notes are a topic on which people write entire books. I first learned them through our AVID program at my school, and our whole district adopted it as a

Annie Bain, a senior majoring in theological studies and art history, barely passed her math requirements for college. She ended her course with a D, proving that math is not her academic strength.

She admits that she never sought help even though tutoring was made available to students through the student union. "It was always about making choices: spending time on the studies that meant something to me or working towards comprehending a subject I would hopefully never see again," she says with a smile.

Her experience with algebra is not uncommon. Of the over 2,000 students who took algebra during that spring, less than 50 percent finished their class with a score of C or higher.

Dr. Michael Moore, the dean of students at her college, nods in recognition. "Nationally, the single greatest academic barrier to student success is mathematics," he says.

Lines indicate what the teacher wants chunked

As a result, her school has decided to develop an unconventional solution to this problem. Rather than use traditional teaching methods to communicate the content, they are allowing computers to teach for them.

Students now work at their own pace, sitting at desktops that are loaded with content that they can access individually. The computers are housed in a 5,800 square-foot space, a "math emporium," that allows students to avoid traditional lecture and whole-class instruction, relying instead on computerized differentiation. The pilot program started with algebra, but the intent is to roll out the model on a wider scale to reflect other subjects.

The idea itself came from an educator at Virginia Tech in 1997. With budget cuts looming and enrollment on the rise, Virginia Tech saw this as an opportunity to increase achievement. After all, the model allowed for students to problem-solve independently and get instant feedback on their work.

Some educators are pushing back on the model, unsure of its effectiveness. Change can be hard to embrace in any industry. However, according to Carolyn Jarmon, the vice-president for the National Center for Academic Transformation, the program is not only effective, but helps bring down the costs of math programs.

Based on the results seen in Bain's program, other universities are considering adopting the math emporium model as well.

The hope is that, eventually, the algebra pass rate at Bain's school will increase to 75 percent and that fewer and fewer students will have to repeat the class. This could translate into savings for the school and the students.

"In my gut," says Dr. Moore, "I know this has to work."

FIGURE 5.2

Many students worldwide strive to reach academical success, and nationwide, math is the number one barrier. Teachers and proffesors found a way that is becoming more and more common. This program includes a huge emporium (5,800 square feet) where Algebra students learn at their own speed and acquire feedback more efficiently from teachers in the lab. This concept, first developed in 1997, proved to increase student grades, and will soon be able to be Used for other courses. Professers are concerned whether this will work or not, but they are reassured that this will help. Dr. Moore firmly believes "In my gut, this has to work."

FIGURE 5.3

note-taking and comprehension technique. Basically, they are dual-entry journals with one side indicating student-developed questions or headings about a reading selection and the other indicating answers to those questions or information related to those sub-topics. The point I want to highlight now, however, is that they also use summary in a section at the bottom. The summary part is key. It's what makes the note-taking also reflective. A student looks back at the questions and answers and creates a summary that serves as both an assessment and a study guide. See Figure 5.5 for an example.

Figure 5.6 is an example from a student-created textbook based on a student's history lesson. For more on Cornell Notes, please see the following resource: The Learning Toolbox, http://coe.jmu.edu/LearningToolbox/cornellnotes.html.

WHAT'S THE BIG IDEA?
Sample paragraphs for summary

1.

"Away from Allenswood, Eleanor's old uncertainty about her looks came back again. She saw herself as too tall, too thin, too plain. She worried about her buckteeth, which she thought made her look horselike. The old teasing began again, especially on the part of Uncle Ted's daughter, "Princess" Alice Roosevelt, who seemed to take pleasure in making Eleanor feel uncomfortable."

Eleanor Roosevelt by William Jay Jacobs

Main idea Eleanor feels insecure about herself   .
(One sentence in your own words)

2.

"People find it curious that those without homes would rather sleep sitting up on benches or huddled in doorways than go to shelters. Certainly some prefer to do so because they are emotionally ill, because they have been locked in before and they are damned if they will be locked in again. Others are afraid of the violence and trouble they may find there. But some seem to want something that is not available in shelters, and they will not compromise, not for a cot, or oatmeal, or a shower with special soap that kills the bugs. "One room," a woman with a baby who was sleeping on her sister's floor once told me, "painted blue." That was the crux of it; not size or location, but pride of ownership. Painted blue."

Homeless by Anna Quindlen

Main idea Home isn't just shelter   .
(One sentence in your own words)

3.

"Besides a place in the record books, the home run race offered Sosa an opportunity to reveal his strength of character. Out of the batting box, he demonstrated the respect and humility that were the very model of sportsmanship. If he finished the season with the most home runs, Sammy said, he would be happy. If McGwire finished with more, he added, he would still be happy! It astonished everyone that Sosa and McGwire seemed to get along so well together. Again and again Soasa maintained that McGwire was a great player, and he wished him the best. In an age when many sports superstars couldn't care less about being an example for others, the conduct of the Cubs' right fielder was refreshing."

Out of the Ballpark by Avery Foster

Main idea Sportmanship is a price which is more worthy than a gold
(One sentence in your own words)
medal

FIGURE 5.4

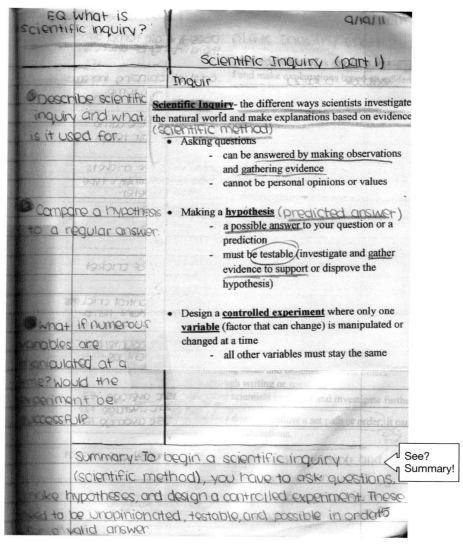

FIGURE 5.5

The Executive Summary

Yet summaries also need not be simple paragraphs or mere sentences in length. The executive summary is a rigorous genre that can be seen echoed in colleges and many careers. The executive summary uses the techniques of summary to indicate a plan or pitch an idea. It's like the combination of summary and argument, but with a calm professional voice.

The cool thing about the executive summary is that it also incorporates many different formats and text structures. It is this visual texture of writing that makes the executive summary so 21st century.

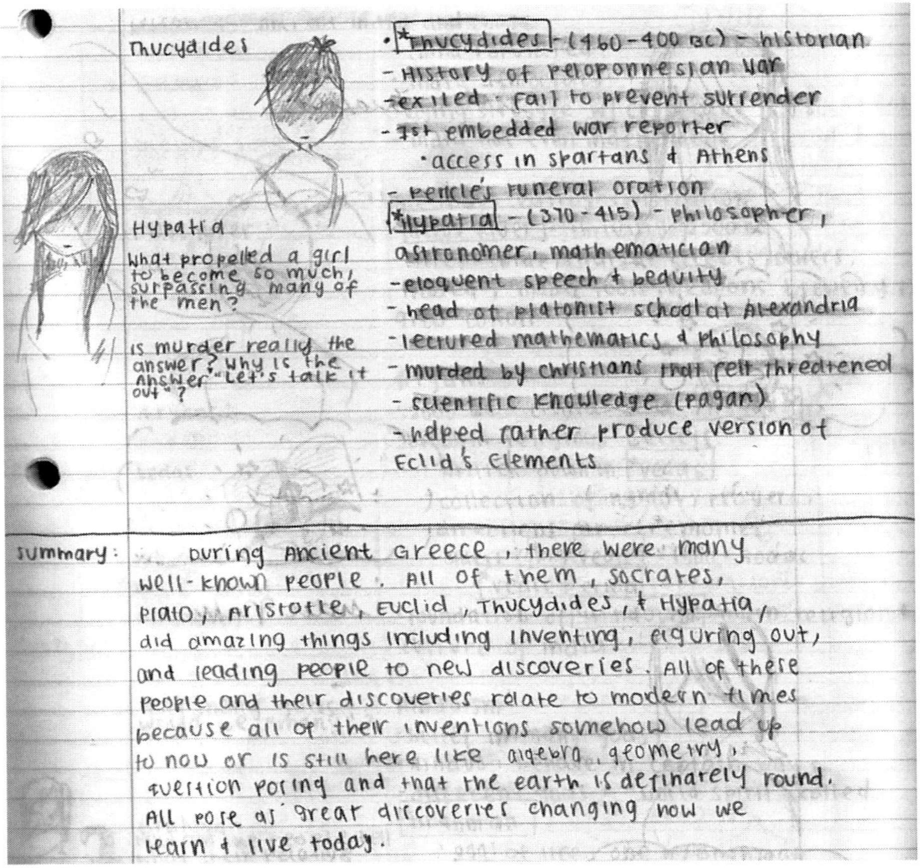

Thucydides

• *Thucydides - (460-400 BC) - historian
- History of Peloponnesian war
- exiled · fail to prevent surrender
- 1st embedded war reporter
  · access in spartans & Athens
- Pericle's funeral oration

Hypatia

What propelled a girl to become so much, surpassing many of the men?

Is murder really the answer? Why is the answer "Let's talk it out"?

*Hypatia - (370-415) - philosopher, astronomer, mathematician
- eloquent speech + beauty
- head of platonist school at Alexandria
- lectured mathematics & philosophy
- murded by christians that felt threatened
- scientific knowledge (pagan)
- helped rather produce version of Eclid's elements

summary: During Ancient Greece, there were many well-known people. All of them, socrates, plato, Aristotle, Euclid, Thucydides, & Hypatia, did amazing things including inventing, figuring out, and leading people to new discoveries. All of these people and their discoveries relate to modern times because all of their inventions somehow lead up to now or is still here like algebra, geometry, question poring and that the earth is definarely round. All rose as great discoveries changing how we learn & live today.

FIGURE 5.6

The point of this kind of writing is best told in real-world role-play. Imagine the student has a boss (you), and must pitch the gist of an issue to you. The purpose is meant to educate you quickly about a topic before your interest and time wanes in the mythical meeting. It must be simple, meaningful, and readable so that anyone can understand the issue and the solution the student may be proposing. An executive summary should do the following:

- Summarize the main points of the issue
- Analyze the most important points
- Recommend a solution.

The rough outline of an executive summary is flexible and should be thought of as sections, not as strict paragraphs per se. It could be this:

I.   Background information
     A. Purpose of report
     B. Scope of the issue
II. Main points
     A. Major findings
     B. Evidence
     C. Methods currently used to solve the problem
     D. How to publicize the issue
III. Recommendations

When writing an executive summary, students should be encouraged to do the following:

1.   Keep language strong and positive.
2.   Write no more than two pages.
3.   Use different text structures: subtitles, bold fonts, bullets, etc.
4.   Write in short, readable paragraphs.

Figure 5.7 is an example of an executive summary that was written by a middle school student for my DARPA/NASA project. As I've written about before, the assignment asked students to conceptualize and research how humans might colonize a planet within one hundred years. The students were broken into various responsibilities within each small group, each reflecting a different perspective to investigate as they worked together to solve the problem: destination, health/medical, ethical issues, political issues, publicity, etc. In the following excerpt, based on the student's research of habitat and environmental sciences, you can see that the student played with text structure and formatting in order to make the executive summary more comprehensible.

This science-based executive summary both informed the audience about the topic and pitched a solution to the problem. In our project, the students themselves role-played as scientists. As such, there was an underlying presence of narrative throughout the whole science unit as well. Some might say it was a multi-genre essay (and they would be right), but it was all based in summary.

To lead up to executive summary, I would scaffold a few lessons in order for them to be up to the task. Here is a brief list of strategies or concepts I would cover before pushing them out on the edge of such a rigorous writing genre:

1.   Text structures—Look at different text-based decisions in your classroom textbook. Why are certain phrases in bold, in italics, in all caps? What makes a word or phrase worthy of being a headline? What is the purpose of indenting text? What are ways to develop a list of items? What kind of text draws your eye immediately? How much text is needed until you, the reader, hit that "I'm phasing out and don't even want to tackle reading more" point?

DARPA: 100 Year Starship Symposium

Habitat and Environmental Science

"We are just an advanced breed of monkeys on a minor planet of a very average star. But we can understand the Universe. That makes us something very special."- Stephen Hawking. Stephen Hawking is correct in this quote. Although, we probably aren't the most special things in the universe, we know what it takes keep the human race alive. In this case we need to go into space to colonize. Track 5 is in charge is in charge of finding solutions to problems like gravity, energy collection, oxygen, and more. We humans may just be a breed of monkeys, but if we work hard enough we can do this and ensure the survival of our race.

One of the most important things for humans to have besides food, water, and oxygen is gravity. Gravity is extremely important for keeping our bodies together and functionable, as said in the previous summary.

Background:

Gravity is caused by 2 main factors. The first is density and mass. Earth has a larger mass and is very dense so it has gravity. The other reason for earth's gravity is rotation. The other reason for earth's gravity is because it rotates on it axis creating stability of the planet and gravity.

Suggestions:

- Artificial gravity (which will actually be centrifugal force)

One way of creating this would be to have one object with some amount of mass rotating inside the ship, which would cause a phenomenon close to gravity. It would pull towards you towards the ship and keep you there. Another pro about centrifugal force is that if anything needed to be fixed on the outside of the ship, you would also stick to the outside of the ship as if you were having a nice stroll in the park on earth.

Problems

- High technology: If there is one flaw in the ship it could cause a major problem
- Where?: The ship would have to be built in space because it would have to be huge. Also the technological abilities can't be done on earth, like the propulsion system and the artificial gravity would have to be built in space.
- Cost: The cost would be astronomically high because of the money necessary to create the artificial gravity and the propulsion system

Gravity on the Colony

There is probably going to be a problem with the gravity level of the colony that we intend to colonize unless it is exactly like earth. For example if we were to colonize on Mars then we would need artificial gravity. Mars has 1/3 of Earth's gravity and although that is enough to live on, side effects of less gravity would still occur and slowly kill us.

FIGURE 5.7A

2. Thesis statement—What will this summary be about?

3. Problem/solution—How do you clearly describe the importance of this problem and how can you explain to someone who doesn't know the topic what the best solution is?

4. How to read data—By reading more and more data in your own content area, students will begin to have some kind of facility in embedding data into their

Solutions:

- One potential solution is using a massive amount of force to rotate the planet. By doing this once the rotation would never stop because space is a vacuum and the rotation would create gravity.

We have the technology to generate the power needed through solar or nuclear power, but we don't have the power to harness it.

- Another solution is to have the colony surrounded by a dome and have to colony rotate.
- This would let us have control over the temperature, weather, and oxygen levels. The final solution is an Orbital Space Colony This would be a colony where we orbit a planet and live in a space colony, or the ship that we would come in. Everything from planting to sleeping to curing sickness would be done on the ship

Oxygen

The most important substance in the entire universe for humans is oxygen. Humans can't go for much more than a minute without oxygen without dying. There are three solutions to get oxygen in space.

1. Separation from Carbon Dioxide- In this technique, you would use a solution like lithium peroxide to separate the carbon from the oxygen. Then humans breathe in the oxygen and the only thing left is the carbon, which can then be recycled.
2. Separation from water: In this tactic we would bring lots of water with us and separate the oxygen from the hydrogen. This is successfully being used on the International Space Station.
3. Plants and Human Loop- This is where humans exhale carbon dioxide and the plant inhales carbon dioxide. The plant then exhales oxygen and we inhale it. Then the process starts again. This way we also help the plants survive so they can produce for us in this never ending loop.
4. Carry what you need- This plan is where all of the oxygen needed is brought from earth and stored people rely on that to breathe.

Energy Supplies and Harnessing

Possible Sources

FIGURE 5.7B

own writing. What kinds of transition words or punctuation are used to integrate data into text? (I will note here that ELA is responsible for teaching punctuation marks, grammar, etc. However, by alerting students to the possible uses of these marks in your own content area, it highlights the fact that targeted choices of punctuation are needed in every subject.)

5. The importance of visuals—How can images be used to highlight your message and not distract from the theme or main idea?

-Geothermal Energy: We could drill into the planets core to get energy.

-Hydroelectric Energy: If we melt the ice caps and have the water run. Then we use the power of the running water to create electricity.

-Solar Energy: Harnessing energy through a solar panel from our largest energy source ever, the sun. The only problem is that we would have to wipe dust off of the panel every couple of hours.

-Nuclear Fission: If we use fission to power our ship we could use that technology on the planet to make energy.

-Wind Energy: Using the wind to turn a turbine, which produces energy.

 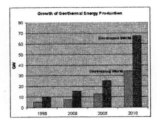 

Recommendations:

I suggest that we use artificial gravity on our space ship to stop most of the effects of micro gravity and then build a dome on the planet. However, if we manage to make the planet rotate faster then the dome wouldn't be necessary. In terms of oxygen, I believe that we have to use a combination of methods 1, 2, 3, and some of 4. This way if a plant dies then we can separate the oxygen from carbon dioxide. If that fails then we can get oxygen from water. If all else fails then we still have the small amount of oxygen stored in a tank. The best energy source is solar energy (from the sun), wind energy (from turbines), and geothermal energy (from the heat of the planets core). All three of these energy sources are reliable and can be used in multiple conditions.

These all seem like great solutions, but to carry these solutions out we would need both funding and good publication. It takes 10,000 dollars to bring one pound of material into orbit around Earth, so we would need a budget billions of dollars. We, the advanced monkeys of Earth, can do this, but we need to be united on this project. We, the advanced monkeys of Earth, also have to think of one thing that is crucial to the mission, "Which planet is our colony going to be on?"

FIGURE 5.7C

TABLE 5.1 Sample Rubric for Scoring Summaries

Does it state the main idea of the reading (article, primary source, textbook, etc.)?

Does it identify completely the most important details that support the main ideas?

Is it written in the student's own words except for quotations?

Does it express the underlying meaning of the article (the big picture), not just the superficial details?

Scoring Summaries

When scoring summary paragraphs, all you need is an easy checklist of requirements. It only takes a quick skim to evaluate the writing quality. A simple way to go would be to create strips of rubrics that can be quickly filled out and attached to a submission. To make it really simple, the following rubric is designated to indicate Y or N, a 1 or a 2. If all requirements are met, the student receives a 4. An example is shown in Table 5.1.

The summary is a stand-alone genre that can be used for any content, but when combined with other genres it is even more real-world. After all, just as I am advocating that content should not be so segregated and categorized, so am I advocating for more blended genres, multi-genres, in every classroom.

For more information on summary writing, check out the following links:

- Drew University On-Line Resources for Writers (http://users.drew.edu/~sjamieso/summary.html)
- Santa Rose JC English Department Online Writing Lab (http://srjcwriting center.com/summaries/summaries.html).

6

The Multi-Genre Genre

I really?

I know as adults we do this but

> Multigenre writing is a good fit for today's active students, as it both capitalizes on student need for variety and recognizes new literacies . . . Despite the seeming chaos, there is valuable energy, spontaneity, and creativity in the process.
>
> (Sherri Larson)

Writing in an uncategorized, blended-genre kind of way allows teachers to do everything they love, everything they know is important, and then some. According to Tom Romano, author of *Blending Genre, Altering Style: Writing Multi-genre Papers*,

> A multigenre paper arises from research, experience, and imagination. It is not an uninterrupted, expository monolog nor a seamless narrative nor a collection of poems. A multigenre paper is composed of many genres and subgenres, each piece self-contained, making a point of its own, yet connected by theme or topic and sometimes by language, images and content. In addition to many genres, a multigenre paper may also contain many voices, not just the author's.

Multi-genre projects and essays allow a student to weave in prose, recipes, poems, dramatizations, expository elements, visuals, and more into a creation that more vividly demonstrates the messiness of true thinking.

Utilizing multi-genre possibilities allows teachers to:

- Continue to teach narrative, a subject that teachers know is incredibly valuable and applicable in today's world;
- Weave in argument, information, fact, and evidence;
- Integrate other content into our classrooms;
- Allow products to be truly multi-modal, reflecting different interests and abilities in their students.

In a Common Core world where innovative thinking is being encouraged, allowing students to create a multi-genre project and essay gives them academic permission to think outside the box. It is the all-encompassing writing that blends and embraces the best of all genres. And it is because of its respect for all subjects and styles that the multi-genre essay is so 21st century.

The Case for Writing Desegregation

Teaching in a segregated way does a disservice to how life beyond school will actually be. So many genres bleed into each other throughout our adult day, yet school continues to put writing genres into little boxes. Frankly, I'm jealous of the authenticity permitted elementary teachers. In fact, the transition to Common Core will most likely be a smoother transition for them. After all, an elementary teacher teaches all the subjects and can pull from one to support the other.

However, by the time students get to the middle and secondary levels, we teach individual subjects in a very categorized way, and it doesn't necessarily benefit the learner. Every room categorizes subjects, and every quarter categorizes lessons. But with categorization comes a lack of transfer.

For instance, in ELA, we've taught persuasive writing one quarter, narrative another, literary analysis, and then summary (or some such similar order). In math, we've taught fractions one unit, decimals the next, one unit building on the other but disallowing the time or the guidance to include how math applies to other subjects or to life outside of school. In history, the pace of teaching is just as intense and teachers struggle with ways to include any content other than their own. Let's face it, look at the seventh grade world history curriculum. What is it? From 400BC to 1400AD for *all* civilizations? That's nuts. It's rich and wonderful, but how does a teacher have an opportunity to weave in other subjects? The answer can be found in writing. Writing is universal, and while it's hard, the routine must change to encourage a more multi-genre format. In fact, multi-genre writing is the most authentic writing of them all.

Only if we break down the walls between subjects will we be able to truly guide students to transfer what they learn from class to class and from school to the world beyond.

With that in mind, I began setting writing categorization in my crosshairs in order to disband the practice, at least in my own classroom. As a result, I'm finding that the philosophical challenges of transitioning to the Common Core are not quite so daunting because, like elementary teachers, I can pull from one genre to support another.

To begin to dismantle the metaphorical writing genre boxes, I started to examine my units and analyze what the components were for each. My goal was to infuse other subjects or genres into each in order to break down the walls in a more blended, and more real-world, way.

I developed a little chart (Table 6.1) that listed some of the units I did during the school year and their elements. I then looked at them critically to see what I could do to add layers of curriculum to each.

As I've said, multiple genres are all around us. That's why it's so important to be including writing in all subjects. If we are desirous of our students to transfer knowledge to the real world beyond school, then we have to incorporate the skills and strategies that are used in the real world. That means writing. A quick exercise

TABLE 6.1 Writing Units I've Taught Over the Years

	Narrative	Informa-tional	Argument	Visuals	Interdisci-plinary Content	Technology
TED conference unit	X	X	X	X	X	X
DARPA/NASA project unit	X	X	X	X	X	X
Book trailers unit	X		X	X		X
Radiolab NPR project	X	X			X	X
Global Shakespeare project	X			X	X	X
Fan fiction unit	X	X		X	X	X

TABLE 6.2 Log of Writing Genres Noticed Throughout the Day

Genre Noticed	Time of Day/Reference
Narrative	12:01 text from Kenna telling me about how her Friday night was
Argument	
Summary	
Analysis	
Informational	

that might be useful is in analyzing the kinds of genres that pop up in the world around us.

Using a simple log (Table 6.2), students and teachers can recognize the different genres at any time during a single day period. If they see or read any kind of descriptive informational text, they can indicate what it was. If they read a form of persuasive text, like an advertisement, campaign speech, or even a text from a peer trying to convince them to eat lunch behind the gym, they can check that off too. And if they read any kind of personal narrative, personal experience, or personal information they can take note of them too.

Middle school science teacher and member of the Teacher Leaders Network Marsha Ratzel says the following about asking her students to write in a more multi-genre way:

My writing quality would be centered around how clearly the message is conveyed and the tools they used to convey their point. I spend lots of time having students look at non-fiction science books . . . drawing attention to how these professional authors use sidebars, pictures, diagrams, graphs and so on to reinforce the point they are making in their writing. I try to drive home the idea that if a professional needs to do that, so do you.

Ratzel brings the outside world into her science classroom by highlighting the use of multi-genre writing as it relates to science. It makes her STEM classroom more authentic and real-world. Furthermore, it is this infusion of different textures and techniques typically included in real-world informational writing genre that makes it multi-genre.

Multi-genre writing is also simply about ensuring that a student is displaying their knowledge of one's content in ways that aren't simply a straightforward, single-genre, flat essay. Rod Powell, a high school history teacher and member of the Center For Teaching Quality's New Millennium cohort, says that:

I try to make my assignments relevant to students and "spin" them in a way to capture interest. For example, my classes completed a cooperative project in which they wrote songs about life during the Black Death. I pitched myself as a record company mogul who could make them incredibly rich and famous if they could write the one song that would sell. Requirements included:

- A research component
- A written rough draft of lyrics
- Cover art for a CD case
- Revised lyrics
- Recorded song produced in GarageBand
- And appropriate rubrics were used to assess work as it progressed.

Powell's history unit clearly interweaves genres and modalities in order to make his unit more applicable. Because of the intricacy of the unit, he addresses a more Common Core expectation that genres are blended, reflecting the world outside of school in a deeper way.

Multi-genres are all around us, every day, mashed together in a melting pot of literacy. To tease them apart and to only teach them in a categorized way would be doing a disservice to authenticity.

The Common Core recognizes that writing genres are all related and inter-twined. This works to the benefit of all subjects because no matter the content, many writing genres can be utilized to communicate that content. Of course, the Common Core Standards highlight argument, and argument, the structured format of convincing and explaining using evidence, can be employed by any content area.

But there are other genres too that can be used to fulfill this requirement of writing in every subject. There's narrative, there's analysis, there's summary, there's informational, and more. The key is to quit separating them and instead use them all. Sure, we've deconstructed each writing genre and teased them apart into separate categories in an attempt to teach them in a controlled compartmentalized fashion, but writing, really good writing, weaves elements of them all together.

Multi-genre writing is like braiding hair. Each strand creates a stronger whole, and repeats throughout the piece, ducking and weaving, and bringing its own highlights to the intricacies of the overall essay (Figure 6.1).

And weaving writing genres together also means not only that other subjects can tap into multiple genres, it means that ELA teachers can bring more content from other subjects into the writing that they specifically teach.

I have mentioned earlier in this book that I recently designed a mock TED.com conference at my school (see Appendix A). For those of you not familiar with TED.com, TED stands for Technology, Entertainment, and Design. It is an online archive of speakers who are the best at their particular niche, whether it is cell animation or app design or puppetry. If the person was selected to speak at one of the national or regional TED conferences, then their speech is available, online, for free, to the masses. It's democratization of information at its best.

Now, when analyzing these speeches by breaking them down into their components, my students and I could better see the truth about them all: that many of them are, in fact, multi-genre essays. Some are about science, some about history, some focus on the arts, some on politics or philosophy. Each involves some sort of memoir (a form of narrative) informational writing, persuasive strategies,

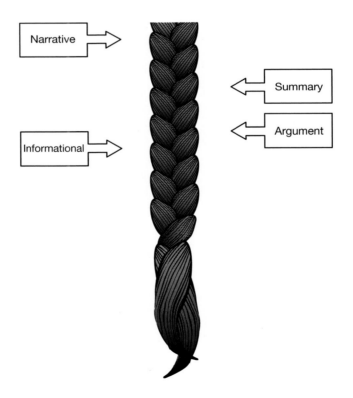

FIGURE 6.1

and visuals. The bottom line is, they all use multiple genres to communicate their content.

With every speech we view, my students fill out a template in order to begin familiarizing themselves with the structure of these speeches. However, it isn't just the structure I want to point out to them. It's also the use of a variety of genres that make up any one given speech. Let's take a look at a few in particular.

Adora Spivak was 12 years old at the time she presented to audiences in 2010. If you examine the transcript of her speech you will notice that she incorporates many genres in order to prove her main idea (www.ted.com/talks/adora_svitak. html). Following are notes from a student based on the 8:14 minute speech:

Name: Adora Spivak
Title: What Adults Can Learn From Kids
Date Performed: 2010
Visual Used: Prezi-like presentation
Theme: Give us some credit! Adults can learn from kids
Was Evidence Used and Cited? Yes
Was There Original Thought and Commentary? Yes
Did She Use Memoir? Yes
Did She Use Persuasive Techniques? Yes
Was There a Call to Action? Yes.

Then there's Terry Moore's 2:57 minute speech, "How to tie your shoes" (www.ted.com/talks/lang/en/terry_moore_how_to_tie_your_shoes.html). Figure 6.2 shows some other notes filled out. Figure 6.3 shows student notes filled out based on Jim Toomey's 14:15 minute speech.

So, as we discovered, whether they are three minutes or twenty-three minutes, you can see that they all include elements of all the genres, but their content differs from speech to speech. There's no reason why, after studying a number of the TED speeches that focus on one's specific content, the students can't mimic the format of the speech itself, but center their arguments on proving an equation, a hypothesis, a philosophy, or perhaps an art form.

They bring in personal narrative, where they first discovered their interest in the topic. They inform the audience of their expertise and describe what is necessary to understand their topic. There is a persuasive advocacy spin that sells a solution or call to action to the audience. Each speech you watch has informational facts and original commentary. Each has graphics and visuals of some kind as well: some use puppetry, others use dance, most use some kind of video, PowerPoint, or other presentation software. This reflects a far more authentic and organic way of writing and, in this case, speaking.

Of course, it's not a math teacher's job to teach elements of narrative or argument, but it is their job to assign writing and to know enough about that genre to assess it. In the very least, it would help teachers see eye to eye a little more in the efforts it takes to accomplish their goals. At best, it makes teachers of other subjects stronger themselves in the skills it takes to communicate their subjects, and that is their job.

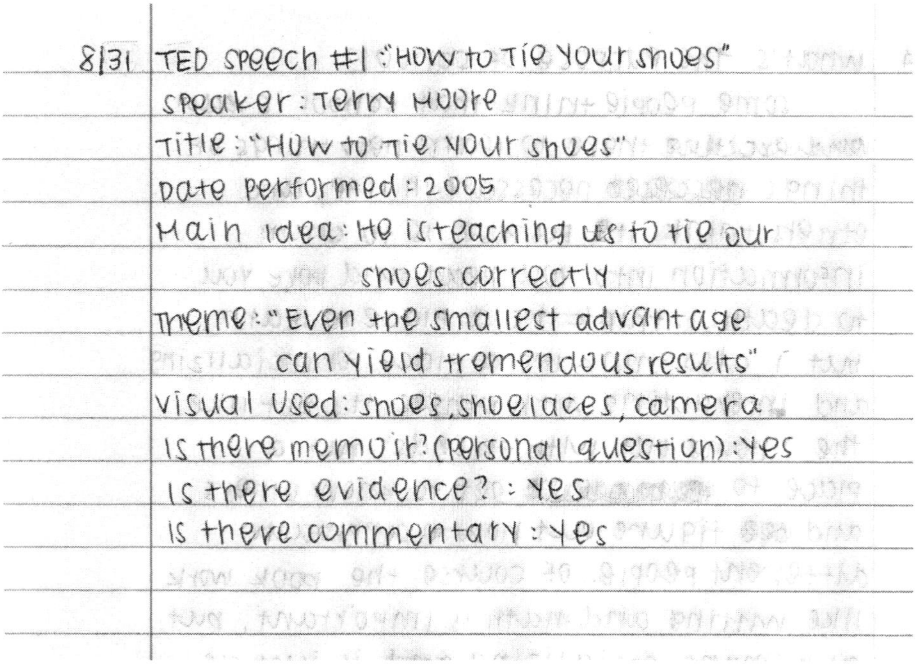

8/31　TED speech #1: "How to tie your shoes"
Speaker: Terry Moore
Title: "How to tie your shoes"
Date performed: 2005
Main idea: He is teaching us to tie our
　　　　　　shoes correctly
Theme: "Even the smallest advantage
　　　　can yield tremendous results"
Visual used: shoes, shoelaces, camera
Is there memoir? (personal question): Yes
Is there evidence?: Yes
Is there commentary: Yes

FIGURE 6.2

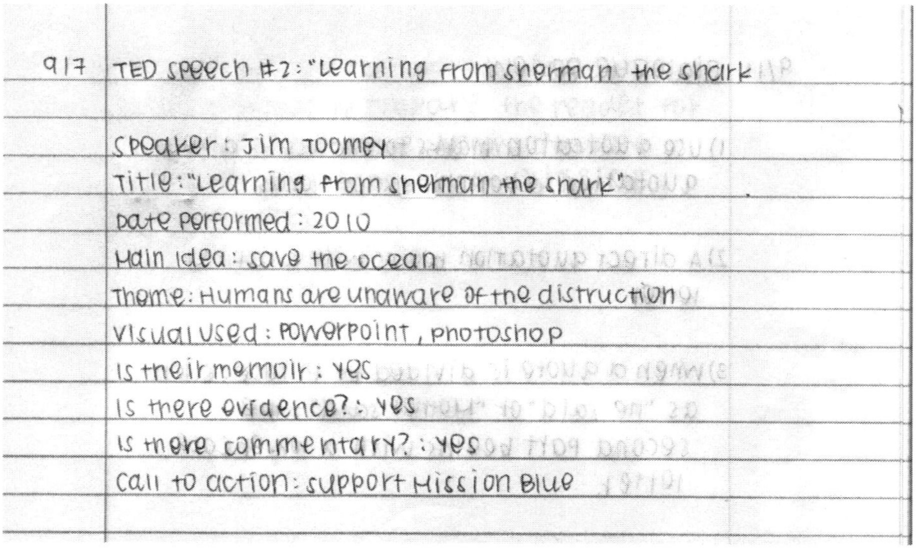

9/7　TED speech #2: "Learning from Sherman the shark"

Speaker: Jim Toomey
Title: "Learning from Sherman the shark"
Date performed: 2010
Main idea: Save the ocean
Theme: Humans are unaware of the distruction
Visual used: PowerPoint, photoshop
Is their memoir: Yes
Is there evidence?: Yes
Is there commentary?: Yes
Call to action: support Mission Blue

FIGURE 6.3

Teaching in a more uncategorized way starts with developing a fundamental understanding of all the individual genres and their components. From there, it's about examining how different elements can be used universally, and how others are more targeted in nature.

In other words, many writing genres share characteristics found in other writing genres, and that makes multi-genre teaching easier for you and more comprehensible for students. The fact that many writing genres share features is important to know, because as a teacher it saves you time in your instruction. For instance, a thesis statement is needed in almost every genre of writing, sans narrative. Evidence is also needed in almost any genre. It's in the form of either textual evidence, data, or personal experience. In fact, by using the checklist in Table 6.3, a teacher can guide a discussion with students that makes the argument—don't tell them ahead of time—that all of the elements listed can be integrated into *any* genre.

Look at the chart in Table 6.3. I hand out a blank one to my ELA students and have them fill it in (see Appendix F), but I've filled it in for you to get an understanding of just how many writing genres and their elements overlap to begin with. Of course, you can argue for or against any of these elements to be included or not in a particular genre. The important thing is that if a teacher who doesn't teach writing sees that, say, hooks are expected in many forms of writing, perhaps that teacher will then hold students to that expectation as well.

TABLE 6.3 Overlapping Elements of Different Writing Genres

	Narrative	Summary	Argument	Analysis	Informational
Hook	X		X	X	
Background Information	X		X	X	X
Thesis Statement			X	X	X
Tag (Title, Author, Genre)		X		X	
Main Topic Sentence		X	X	X	X
Evidence			X	X	X
Commentary			X	X	X
Transition Words	X	X	X	X	X
Voice	X				
Sentence Variety	X	X	X	X	X
Conventions	X	X	X	X	X
Figurative Language	X				
Plot	X				
Rising Action	X				
Exposition	X				
Setting	X				
Characters	X				
Conflict	X		X		
Falling Action	X				
Resolution	X				
Theme	X	X			
Counterarguments			X		
Call To Action/Solution			X		

The fact is that any assignment, any project, can integrate multiple genres, and should.

The Ultimate Multi-Genre Writing Projects: Websites and Apps

Now, there are many different informal and formal writing assignments that can be seeded into a multi-genre project. The point is, after all, to take the most appropriate styles of writing, whatever they may be, and match them to the topic or theme of the overall project.

There are many different kinds of writing that students can choose from in creating something more blended in nature. Table 6.4 is a chart, from a workbook I wrote for Teacher Created Resources, that gives some options for students.

However, as the subheading of this section tells you, the ultimate, real-life multi-genre writing projects are in creating both websites and apps. Both relate to our goal of real-world, authentic assessment. And both are ripe with multiple genres in their development.

Look at Table 6.5. The fact is, that having the students build simple, straight-forward websites is unavoidably multi-genre and, in so doing, extremely Common Core. Having students build simple apps is also a skill with which students can leave your class feeling proudly applicable to the world outside of school. Building these projects is also amazingly engaging as artifacts for some project-based learning in any content area.

TABLE 6.4 Blended Genre Options for Students

Written (Linguistic)	Visual (Non-Linguistic)	Other
Campaign Speech	Ad	Directions
Character Sketch	Family Tree	Recipe
Dialogue	Greeting Card	Quiz
Essay	Website	How-To Guide
Fable or Fairy Tale	Picture Book	List
Poetry	Map	Song
Diary Entry	Postcard	Dance
Blog	Movie Poster	Board Game
Memoir	Diorama	Computer Game
News Article	Flipbook	Reader's Theater
Op-ed Piece	Lego Structure	Podcast
Petition	Statue	Video
Advocacy Essay	Comic Book	Monologue
Letters	Comic Life (using iLife suite)	PowerPoint
Review	Prezi	
Script	PowerPoint	
Glossary	Blueprint (using Google SketchUp)	
Narrative		
Interview		
Legend		
Letter of Complaint		
Summary		

TABLE 6.5 Elements of Websites and Apps

	Websites	Apps
21st Century communication	X	X
Text written in prose	X	X
Tags	X	X
Menus	X	X
Formattable text structure (bullets, font differentiation, headlines, etc.)	X	X
Images	X	X
Multimedia	X	X
Interactive elements (quizzes, surveys, etc.)	X	X

Following is an example of a student website that was created as the end project of my DARPA/NASA unit. The unit itself utilized the executive summary format but wove in other writing genres as well as a scientific, interdisciplinary focus. Check out the Group "Syntax Error" website (http://93138756.nhd.weebly.com).

The project itself was for small groups to collaborate on the umbrella topic based on a 2011 NASA and DARPA conference. (For more on this unit, see the Appendix G checklist.)

You'll notice that there are pictures, video, even quotes on the process from the authors. Each student wrote an executive summary that also included persuasive word choice, data, and prose. There is textured writing in the form of bullets, bolded texts, different fonts, etc. One student developed a game, another created art using Photoshop. The website housed it all.

The important thing to note here is that I am not a science teacher. Nevertheless, I developed a unit that emphasized scientific content as much as it required high levels of multi-genre writing to communicate that science.

Another unit that culminated in the creation of a website was my most recent TED unit (see above). As I described earlier in this book (see Chapter 3), the TED unit divided up multiple tasks and combined them into one whole collaborative project. One student created a National Public Radio Radiolab-esque segment. One student created an infographic. Another created a Prezi. The fourth created a website to house all of the projects as well as the collaborative essay to which each student contributed.

In terms of producing the actual written component, I used a jigsaw technique to break down the task. Student #1 wrote the introduction to the essay, which included the thesis statement that took an agreed-upon stand on a particular issue. Student #2 wrote the background information and made sure to include cited evidence as to the existence of the real-world problem that needed to be solved. Student #3 wrote a body paragraph that included more textual evidence, perhaps brought up a counterargument that pushed back on their findings. Last, Student #4 wrote the call to action, a section that focused on what the audience/reader should do to help solve the problem. These sections became natural tabs on the website which, for me, made it very easy to delineate who did what, and as a consequence, very easy to score.

Each student submitted his or her own research to add to the resources page. Each student sent the web designer suggested art or links. Each student was responsible for his or her own tab's writing quality.

One such example is this one, from a group that decided to focus on racism in education (http://racismineducation.weebly.com/brandons-page.html). Again, like the DARPA/NASA website above, this one has all the elements that qualify it for multi-genre status.

In order to build apps, I have discovered a really easy drag-and-drop program called iBuildApp.com. I'm not an expert in coding. In fact, I would have no idea where to begin, but this easy program allows me to create a free account (as long as I don't care about monetizing my app) for either the Web, an iPhone, or an Android. It allows you to create tabs and type text into each page of an app, much like a website provides.

In 2013, my ELA class began using iBuildApp in order to create apps helping to pitch and inform students about Shakespeare's *A Midsummer Night's Dream.* I first spent my spring break familiarizing myself with the program by building an app with my then 6-year-old son. He wanted to create a "Ben's Dragon University" app, where each page was a dragon that he invented. Figure 6.4 is a screenshot of a page in progress (6-year-old spelling included).

From there, I introduced the program to my teenage students and let them take off running. With them working in small groups, I set deadlines when different text was due. Different students in each group were responsible to produce different pages for the app. There was one page on the history of Shakespeare, another on the plot of *A Midsummer Night's Dream,* another was on a history of past productions, and so on.

Now, just imagine that your app isn't about literature. Instead, it is about your content area. Perhaps students in every small group designed an app on different topics from the school year. Perhaps you use it as a reflection on the whole school year. Nevertheless, building apps is a vessel for any content. Just look at the iTunes Store and type in your subject to see what I mean.

Both projects became multi-genre units that blended writing and inter-disciplinary content into an overall series of pages and assessments that excited the students and encouraged a real deep learning about all topics. These units were real-life. They were authentic. And they were Common Core.

To read more on multi-genre writing, check out the following resources:

- *Blending Genre, Altering Style: Writing Multigenre* by Tom Romano.
- *A Teacher's Guide to the Multigenre Research Project* by Melinda Putz.

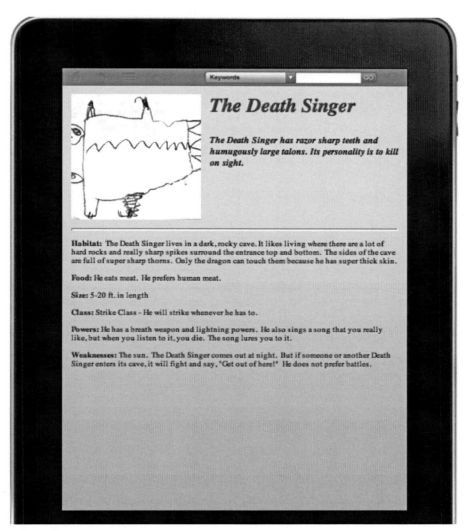

FIGURE 6.4

7

Techniques to Teach Writing That Work

> Striving to strengthen their teaching, accomplished teachers critically examine their practice, seek to expand their repertoire, deepen their knowledge, sharpen their judgment and adapt their teaching to new findings, ideas and theories.
>
> (The National Board for Professional Teaching Standards)

Thinking about my toolbox of writing strategies is like going into a huge walk-in closet, the kind with the dry-cleaner revolving rack. You press a button and one strategy maneuvers with a soft grind, coming to a stop in front of you. Will this strategy be the perfect one to use for teaching this draft? No. Press again, and this time another tactic moves into place. Will this one get the idea across to more learners? Hmmm . . . Let's look for yet another approach. Ah! Perfect.

As a language arts teacher, I have the luxury of having such a closet from which to pull. But in all honesty many of the most long-running and successful strategies don't have to wait for the precisely perfect stage in the writing process to be used. In fact, the best strategies don't need special set-ups or scaffolds. They can be whipped out during any class, for any piece of writing, even those produced in other content areas.

However, not all teachers have the benefit of years of strategy collecting, at least not in writing. So I wanted to devote this chapter to the general strategies that work. These are the approaches that teachers have taught me, shared with me, and used in their own classrooms. These are some of the best strategies from some of the best writing teachers around. These are also the strongest strategies and tactics I've developed for my own students through the years that I feel would benefit any subject. For teachers of different content areas, for new teachers, and for teachers looking to add to their awesome closet, this chapter's for you.

The Big List of Writing Strategies for Use in Any Classroom

Color-Coding

Color-coding is a way to visualize paragraph structure. It isn't meant to be a scaffold that students use throughout their K12 education, but it is meant to get them on the road towards accomplishing a certain level of written expectation. An educator named Jane Schaffer developed it. Basically, it asks a student to use a simple paragraph outline, aligning each component of the paragraph with a color. The outline is as follows:

The Topic Sentence should be highlighted, underlined, or written in BLUE.
The Evidence/Concrete Details/Facts should be in RED.
The Commentary/Original Thoughts should be GREEN.
The Conclusion/Transition Sentence should be BLUE again.

By assigning colors to specific written elements, a student (from the lowest level of learner to the highest level of learner) can easily recall what comes next and analyze what might be missing from a peer's work or from their own. The colors help to embed the pattern that makes up the structure of writing. Color-coding doesn't just work with any topic, it also works with many levels of learners, from honors to at risk, from EL to RSP.

An offshoot of color-coding is to also use shapes to connect a student with the writing. For instance, a student might write a simple draft of a scientific argument, but then put a cloud shape around the thesis statement or a square around a fact found from their experimentation. Perhaps they put a star next to their hypothesis, but a squiggly line underneath their actual findings. Through using color and shapes, a student interacts with both the writing structure and the content.

Figure 7.1 is an example of a science-based paragraph by a ninth grader that uses a similar method of text interaction.

You can also fool around with your own color and shape combinations. The key, however, is to be consistent. Have students highlight their outline in the same color and shape combinations as their rough drafts. Elaine Keysor, a wonderful history teacher in Dublin, CA, uses this strategy often in the writing she requires from her secondary school students. She says,

One of my favorite essay writing strategies is color-mapping. Thesis statement is red, supporting ideas are green, evidence is blue and commentary is yellow. I have wordless color-mapped examples of essays, rubrics 1–4 . . . Students

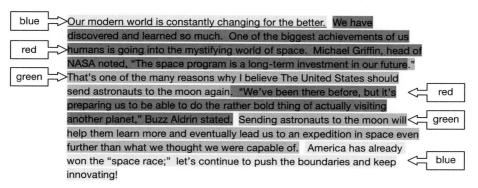

FIGURE 7.1

analyze example essays from the point of view of the components required. It's always an ah–ha! moment for students.

To learn more about Jane Schaffer's methods of teaching writing, go to http://curriculumguides.com/about-us.

Strategies for Embedding Evidence

Students do not come to the table with the knowledge of how to integrate evidence into an informational paragraph. We have to teach them certain tricks to embed evidence in a high–level, sophisticated way.

Teaching students to use evidence can be challenging because secondary students in particular can be stubborn. They can believe that their argument is evidence enough. But it's not. They need to prove it too. Simply stating that "Global warming is a problem that will affect us all" is not enough. Students have to back up that statement with facts.

Suzie Menerey, a dear colleague and an award-winning teacher, created a mantra of sorts for her students to reinforce the need for evidence and lots of it. She developed four statements that act as a guide for evidential writing:

"State it. Prove it. Defend it. Win it!!!!"

This then becomes almost a simple outline for a student to use in their writing. The main topic sentence is the "State it." The evidence is the "Prove it." The commentary is the "Defend it." And finally, the conclusion is what needs to bring it all home so that the student can "Win it."

I have seen her passionately state this, fist slamming on the table, twinkle in her eye, challenging her students to convince her. "Kids love the simplicity of it," she says. "They remember it and use it as their guide to supporting a thesis, and in answering questions in literature." Clearly, however, this chant is not limited to language arts alone.

But getting students into the habit of incorporating evidence isn't enough. We then, as a universal teaching movement, need to consistently insist on how to weave in evidence in a more eloquent way. When we teach students how to embed evidence into a written paragraph, it begins with providing sentence stems to ease them into a more smooth, transitioning language. A paragraph without these aids can read choppy and lower level than the content indicates. A paragraph that includes transitions between the main argument and the evidence reads at a far higher level.

Following is a short-answer essay written in a computer elective class that illustrates the before and after of using sentence stems.

Before sentence stems:

I agree with the author of the article, "Is Google Making Us Stupid?" Google is NOT making us stupid. The internet has changed the world, and unimaginable information is now available in a matter of seconds prompted by the click of a mouse. Google offers free and inlimited [sic] resources. It is changing the way our brains work. "Google is the new technology. The internet contains the world's best writing, images, and ideas, all available instantly." Google does a great job granting us access to all of these. You need to ask good questions. You need to use good keywords. The only thing Google is doing to society is opening the minds of people.

After sentence stems (see italicized words and phrases):

I agree with the author of the article, "Is Google Making Us Stupid?" *I strongly agree with the point that* Google is NOT making us stupid. *Of course,* the internet has changed the world, and unimaginable information is now available in a matter of seconds prompted by the click of a mouse. *It's true that* Google offers free and inlimited [sic] resources. *For that reason,* it is changing the way our brains work, but in a good way. *Peter Norgiv, the author of the article, explains it well when he writes,* "Google is the new technology. The internet contains the world's best writing, images, and ideas, all available instantly." *In fact,* Google does a great job granting us access to all of these. *However,* you need to ask good questions and you need to use good keywords. *As a result,* the only thing Google is doing to society is opening the minds of people.

As for how to teach a more quality level of embedding evidence, simply post possible stems on the wall or include them as a handout in the students' writer's notebooks (see more on this strategy in the section headed 'Using a Writer's Notebook', later in this chapter). From there, the key is to recognize them yourself and require their use. See the following section for other sentence stems options.

Strategies for Incorporating Commentary

Now, evidence is one thing, but the real hurdle is in then asking students to tap into their commentary, their original thoughts. It's not as easy for them as it is for us. Therefore, we have to teach them certain scaffolds to help them think about thinking. Teaching metacognition is challenging to many teachers, but there are ways to kick-start the process. From there, it's about consistency. In my last book, I talk a lot about strategies to get kids thinking and writing. I talk about how commentary is like a tickertape that constantly runs, whispering thoughts about the world around you. The trick is to get a student to freeze that tickertape and be able to translate it into writing.

Stacy Lica, a Fellow of the California Writing Project and a high school teacher, says,

For me, the most important skill I teach, bar none, is the idea that you state a claim, give evidence to support your claim, and (most importantly) use commentary to explain how the evidence proves the claim. My students can do the first two parts fairly easily, but when it comes to substantial and effective commentary, they need tons of work. We spend the bulk of our writing time working on commentary/justification because if they can leave my classroom writing stronger commentary, I feel that we were successful. It's the skill that transfers to writing in every area of their lives, academic and personal. Justify why the facts prove your claim.

It's hard to get a secondary student to freeze all those thoughts flitting about their brain and comment on a mathematical equation. It's especially difficult for students who struggle with reading and writing, who don't read often enough or engage with deep enough content to recognize commentary when they see it. For that reason, you need to provide scaffolds for them to select from. In time, perhaps with maturity or more access to academic reading, they will then be able to remove those scaffolds; but as teachers, we should provide some guidance when we can.

I always tell students that a piece of writing, even informational writing, without commentary is flat and dull. They need to inflate it with their thoughts. I call it giving an essay CPR. To trigger commentary, I give them the following choices:

C—Connect to self, the world, the media, etc. Where have you seen this evidence before?

P—Predict. What would happen if . . .?

R—Relate the evidence to a metaphor or commentary. What does the evidence remind you of?

There are other choices too that just don't fit into the nifty acronym:

Q—Questioning. Can you develop a high-level question to ask about the evidence?

E—Evaluation. What is your opinion of the evidence you found?

Figure 7.2 is what this looks like in an informational paragraph, before deep commentary was added.

And Figure 7.3 is the final draft of that same paragraph after the student inserted commentary (and with a little final drafting pixie dust from the spelling and punctuation fairies).

I don't demand students use these specific scaffolds, but the list provides options for those who struggle, who when faced with a blank page, can't seem to tap into the elusive deeper commentary.

A quick commentary work-out would be to give students a quote, perhaps from the textbook or a primary document, and have them develop a single sentence of commentary that predicts, evaluates, relates to it, compares it, or questions (Table 7.1). It becomes a different kind of opening activity and one that highlights the difference between the evidence on the page and the commentary in their brain.

A math teacher can give students, not a quote, but perhaps an equation. A science teacher can give students a hypothesis or principle. In the following case, a history teacher has given students a quote from the Bill of Rights that functions as the evidence. The student has then used the strategies to write different sentences reflecting various strategies of commentary. From there, the student can then select

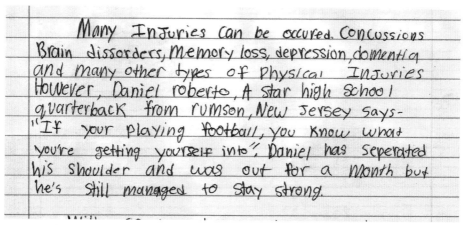

FIGURE 7.2

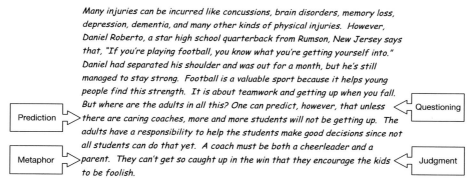

Many injuries can be incurred like concussions, brain disorders, memory loss, depression, dementia, and many other kinds of physical injuries. However, Daniel Roberto, a star high school quarterback from Rumson, New Jersey says that, "If you're playing football, you know what you're getting yourself into." Daniel had separated his shoulder and was out for a month, but he's still managed to stay strong. Football is a valuable sport because it helps young people find this strength. It is about teamwork and getting up when you fall. But where are the adults in all this? One can predict, however, that unless there are caring coaches, more and more students will not be getting up. The adults have a responsibility to help the students make good decisions since not all students can do that yet. A coach must be both a cheerleader and a parent. They can't get so caught up in the win that they encourage the kids to be foolish.

Prediction
Metaphor
Questioning
Judgment

FIGURE 7.3

TABLE 7.1 Quick Commentary Workout

Connect	This makes me think of Martin Luther King's legacy and the rights that he fought for.
Predict	I predict that different cultures and races will use this right to balance out and unite the U.S. We can divide easily as a result of our differences, but the fact is that we aren't restricted from voting due to skin color connects us together.
Relate	The people of the U.S. are like the colors of the spectrum. We're different but when we, as colors, come together, we become one.
Question	Why isn't gender included in this quote?
Visualization	I visualize a blind person managing the voting booths. They don't see color or race when allowing someone to vote.

the commentary he or she feels is most valuable to the overall argument, and embed it into a final draft.

> Evidence: "The right of citizens of the United States to vote shall not be denied or abridged by the United States or any State on account of race, color, or previous condition of servitude."—The Bill of Rights

Figure 7.4 is another example, this one based on a science-related topic. Another strategy a teacher can have students use to create commentary is the dual-entry journal.

COMMENTARY PRACTICE

Quote: "The shape of the plane's wing as it passes through the air creates lower pressure above the wing than beneath it." — The Bernoulli Principle

Connect:	In society almost everywhere I go, I can see something relating to this. In all work atmospheres there is usually and most likely one person that does the most work in a group. And that is just like creating less work for the person next.
Predict:	Using this theory, I can predict that in the near future, scientist or engineers will advanced greatly. This principal can be used to push our technology into a new era not only in planes, but in others as well.
Relate:	I can relate this to almost everything that is airborne. The pressure is always the most underneath, just like a leaf falling down.
Question:	This principle makes me wonder whether or not this will ever contribute to the discovery of hover crafts
Visualization:	I picture this principal as the two wings of the a plane tilted upwards so that the pressure is more beneath the wings.
Judgment:	Because I am very passionate and interested in science, I find this quote or principal very fascinating.

FIGURE 7.4

Dual-Entry Journals

Dual-entry journals are a simple way to set up and get to writing. They are visual, and they can be used for pre-writing or simply as a note-taking template. In terms of producing commentary, however, it is easy to simply assign the two columns to the following categories: "What I Read" and "What's in My Head."

The "What I Read" column asks students to identify and extract textual evidence or factual observations. The "What's in My Head" column asks them to bring their own original thoughts to the evidence by helping them freeze their tickertape at the time they read or observed the piece of information. Figure 7.5 is just such an example of a dual-entry journal based on a music-related article.

Of course, a teacher can have the columns read whatever they need. They can read "Observed/Thought About." They can read "Equation/Application to the World." Whatever. The point is that the one column takes it to a certain level, while the next one takes it that much further.

Modeling

When I first began to write this chapter, I asked colleagues both online and off what was the most valuable tool in their toolbox that they used to teach writing. Every one of them mentioned modeling. This means not only providing models, though that is great too, but also modeling how to write by writing in front of the students.

Modeling is about participating in the class lesson itself. The teacher must provide examples of the assignments he or she asks of the students by writing them in true time. It means writing publicly, in front of the students, in all its messy glory. So let's say you want your students to write a paragraph on justifying a mathematical principle. You would go through the process of constructing your own paragraph on the LCD projector. You'd talk your way through it too: crossing out words you might want to come back to for better choices later, sharing your thought process as you chose what sentence stem you used to lead into a quote or other piece of evidence, thinking aloud about a question that you now may have that can then be used for commentary. Sharing your efforts and your process is a powerful strategy, and one that can be used in any classroom, for any grade level.

Kelly Gallagher, the prolific educator and author, has dedicated a whole book to this topic, called *Write Like This*. It is a valuable book in any professional library. In it, he reminds us that we, the teachers, are the best writers in the classroom, and as such we must be a resource for how students access and communicate our content. When we talk about modeling we are really talking about two things:

1. Providing model pieces of writing *and* talking through why these are model pieces because students aren't necessarily putting together in their heads the reason why an exemplar is chosen as an example.

2. Writing in front of the students and thinking aloud at your own process and decisions as you write the words.

I know this because

Dual Entry: Should Art & Music Be Mandatory?

What I Read:	What's in my head:
"The arts tie us to other cultures and can be enjoyed by everyone..."	I never really made this connection, so I found it really interesting. I agree with the author. I don't know anyone who hates looking/listening to art/music. But making art/music isn't fun for everyone...
"...empty our lives would be without ... paintings ... and the melodic tones of music..."	I myself love music a lot and I can't imagine life without it. Art and music is everywhere and in lots of things.
"...studies have shown that exposing young people to art and music ... fosters academic achievement in core subjects..."	This is really interesting. I do choir, so I wonder if it has helped me in math, or other subjects. This is like a double win.
"helps autistic and developmentally disabled students to grasp mathematical concepts and solve problems."	Music is very enjoyable and apparently it helps your brain comprehend better as well. These students can get help while learning many other things.
"... discipline and enhancing social and communication skills... collaboration."	In my chorus class my teacher likes us to work as a group to get things done while having fun. This helps me meet new people and get exposed to learning new things.

FIGURE 7.5

For many of these students, the closest they will come to a writer is the teacher in the room. They have to be allowed into the process that goes into writing. That's what is so powerful in watching someone write. I know that it can be tough when you have six periods and you find yourself writing something over and over just to model it; but it's fun to look back with the classes at all the drafts and share the evolution of the writing over the course of the day.

Alice Mercer, middle school teacher, blogger, and ed tech advocate, says that she provides examples for her students constantly.

> Ones I write, ones from their fellow students, ones given after they've written so they have models for editing and revising their work. When they see what you are actually asking for, it tends to make a lot more sense to them.

However, just hearing what's expected isn't enough. Provide insight into the process of writing at the level you need for your students to produce. Then provide model pieces, posted all around them in a classroom rich with exemplars. Post correct examples of work, color-coded whenever possible. It not only helps in establishing a standard, but it's a great effort and time saver when kids show up saying they don't know how to do an assignment. Nevertheless, providing exemplars gives them access to standards; modeling how to write those exemplars gives students insight into how to achieve them.

Differentiated Writing Assignments

Give them ways to show understanding in different ways that count. Sure, we assess on writing essays, but can we also assess a skill based on a one to three sentence submission like an exit card, a blog post, or caption? How about as a discussion, debate, or formal conversation that can then be converted into more formal writing if need be? Create opportunities for short written responses. They are less threatening for students and still send the message that writing and communicating content is valued in your classroom.

For example, you can have students create "Think Marks" bookmarks. These are slender pieces of paper where students can write questions, thoughts, vocabulary, summaries, etc. Try a template like the one in Figure 7.6.

By providing them such informal outlets that are less threatening than a formal essay, you are allowing them to prove knowledge of their content while still holding them to the standard of using the written word.

Using a Writer's Notebook

I first started using writer's notebooks in 2004 after a training with America's Choice. I have also seen them in use in such programs as History Alive! Of course, it's a strategy that has been around far longer than that, and you don't have to teach writing in order to see the benefits of having your students develop their own writer's notebooks. A writer's notebook (anything from a spiral notebook to a traditional composition book) is a place for all things written regardless of the content. It's a house for notes, drafts, quickwrites, quickdraws, outlines, etc. It includes a table of contents that gets added to with every assignment and every lesson. In a sense, a writer's notebook is a textbook of both content and writing standards for every class, created by students in collaboration with their teachers. A typical table of contents for a writer's notebook in a science class might look something like Figure 7.7.

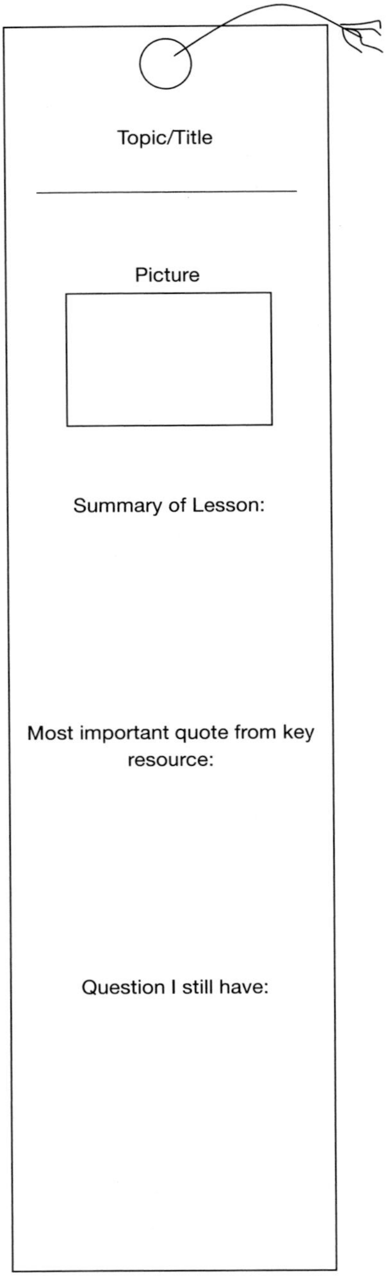

Topic/Title

_____

Picture

Summary of Lesson:

Most important quote from key resource:

Question I still have:

FIGURE 7.6

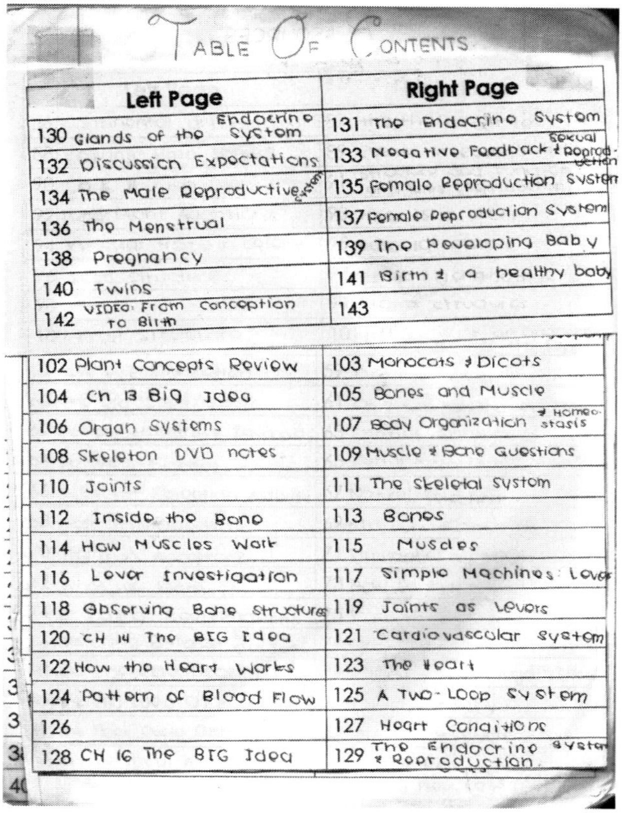

TABLE OF CONTENTS

Left Page	Right Page
130 Glands of the Endocrine System	131 The Endocrine System
132 Discussion Expectations	133 Negative Feedback & Sexual Reproduction
134 The Male Reproductive System	135 Female Reproduction System
136 The Menstrual	137 Female Reproduction System
138 Pregnancy	139 The Developing Baby
140 Twins	141 Birth & a healthy baby
142 Video: From Conception to Birth	143
102 Plant Concepts Review	103 Monocots & Dicots
104 Ch 13 Big Idea	105 Bones and Muscle
106 Organ Systems	107 Body Organization & Homeostasis
108 Skeleton DVD notes	109 Muscle & Bone Questions
110 Joints	111 The Skeletal System
112 Inside the Bone	113 Bones
114 How Muscles Work	115 Muscles
116 Lever Investigation	117 Simple Machines: Lever
118 Observing Bone Structure	119 Joints as Levers
120 CH 14 The BIG Idea	121 Cardiovascular System
122 How the Heart Works	123 The Heart
124 Pattern of Blood Flow	125 A Two-Loop System
126	127 Heart Conditions
128 CH 16 The BIG Idea	129 The Endocrine System & Reproduction

FIGURE 7.7

Each entry represents a page of notes, writing activity, rough draft, or written observation. Each entry represents the writing happening in a content-area classroom.

A great resource for learning more about how to use a writer's notebook in your classroom, regardless of your subject, is *Writer's Notebook: Unlocking the Writer Within You* by Ralph Fletcher.

Blogging

OK, there aren't many silver bullets in education, but I think blogging comes darn close. Giving an academic outlet to write online brings out writers where you may not have seen evidence of one before. Blogging makes assessments transparent; and, let's face it, peer pressure to perform at a certain level can go a long way. Yet blogging can also tap into bravery in a way that writing in class cannot.

Blogging means they don't have to raise their hand in public. In addition, a teacher can create a prompt easily, based on responding not only to a piece of reading but also to a picture or a video. What's turned in can be anywhere from one sentence to five paragraphs. It's up to you, but it definitely seems to demystify participation for many of them.

It's easy to set up a class blog if you don't already have one. Again, many ELA teachers may already be using this resource but, statistically, not as many teachers in other content areas seem to be utilizing this form of communication.

Some districts have deals with programs like My Big Campus or Edmodo, both of which are very Facebook-esque in appearance and format. An individual teacher, however, can easily set up a free website for student blogging using any of the following resources:

- Weebly (www.weebly.com)
- WordPress (http://wordpress.com)
- Kidblog (http://kidblog.org/home).

Kidblog, in particular, is a great place to introduce students to blogging and online communication. The kids can customize their own pages and the teacher has methods to monitor online content and behavior while still creating an environment of transparency. This issue of public writing not only sometimes ups the quality of the student submission but is also vital when teaching digital literacy and online footprints, both of which are lessons all classes should be adopting. Again, any way to universalize a message of high-level writing and critical thinking among all the classrooms is a way to reinforce the lesson.

Accessible Scaffolds

I've written about different scaffolds (various outlines, sentence stems lists, etc.) throughout this book, but I wanted to stress this point again. Accessible scaffolds are supports for students to use at their discretion to help them elevate their writing all by themselves. It's important that all students have access to what they need, whenever they need it, at the tips of their fingers. By providing scaffolds that students are permitted to utilize whenever they need to, you are encouraging independent learning.

Have them keep handouts in their binders or glue resources into their writer's notebooks. These documents can then be accessed anytime a student needs to seek out an answer that has already been covered. This is also a way not to waste time re-teaching a writing skill in lieu of moving ahead with necessary content. Instead, a student can just access the answer when needed.

There are many scaffolds that can be provided that could help their writing. They include, but are not limited to, the following:

How to Ask Different Levels of Questions (From Costa's Levels of Questioning)

Level 1:
    What is . . .?
    When did . . .?
    Who are the main . . .?
    Can you recall . . .?
    Can you list . . .?

Level 2:

How would you compare . . .?
How would you rephrase . . .?
Can you explain . . .?
Which statements support . . .?
Can you identify the main idea of . . .?
How would you summarize . . .?

Level 3:

Why do you think . . .?
What evidence did you find . . .?
Can you make a distinction between . . .?
What inference can you make . . .?
How can you justify . . .?
Can you predict the outcome if . . .?
What changes would you make to solve . . .?

Transitional Stems for Launching into Evidence or Commentary

Of course . . .

In short . . .

Obviously . . .

Nevertheless . . .

As a result . . .

It is true that . . .

However . . .

Therefore . . .

Admittedly . . .

On the other hand . . .

So . . .

I understand that . . .

Yet . . .

To be sure . . .

Although . . .

For this reason . . .

This line shows that . . .

This example of _____ displays that . . .

This quote illustrated that . . .

This states that . . .

This is not unlike . . .

After that . . .

Another key characteristic is . . .

An example of this concept is . . .

In order to understand this (concept) . . .

A person can conclude that . . .

It is clear that . . .

Additionally . . .

This expert states that . . .

One example to support this is . . .

Kinds of Hooks (Ways to Start Essays)

For my book *Project Based Writing*, written for Teacher Created Resources, I created a list in which I "rehooked" a world history essay on the Black Death. You can see the handout in full in Appendix H. However, here is the list of strategies to suggest to students, as well as an example for each:

- **A fact/statistic**—Nearly a third of the population of Europe was killed by the Plague.

- **Tone/mood**—The bodies piled up in the streets of London, untouched, uncared for, mourned by the frightened masses that were left behind wondering when it was going to be their turn to die.

- **Simile/metaphor**—The Black Death swept across the land like a broom, brushing away people as it would dirt.

- **In the middle of the action**—The trebuchet cranked back slowly, then released suddenly, launching the body up and over the walls of the city.

- **Definition**—The Black Death was an unstoppable disease caused by the fleas carried by the rats that cohabitated with the people of Medieval Europe.

- **Dialogue**—"I see there's been no improvement," the apothecary sadly admitted, looking at the small girl trembling and sweating with fever before him.

- **Onomatopoeia**—Sssssss. Sizzle. The fever burned through the victim's body.

- **Staccato three-word lead**—Rats. Sewers. Filth. London was not a city of great cleanliness.

- **Lyrics**—"Ring around the rosie. Pockets full of posies. Ashes, ashes, we all fall down!"

- **Theme**—Some people believed that the Plague was sent to punish the evil on earth, but they would soon learn that the disease knew no such ethics. It did not distinguish its victims.

Lists of Words and Punctuation Options to Create More Complex Sentences

For this, have students list all the ones they can think of and include them in their writer's notebook. Make sure they leave a few rows blank to insert others as ideas occur to them. This then becomes a resource that doesn't have to be taught so much as accessed when needed. See Table 7.2 for an example.

TABLE 7.2 Words and Punctuation to Create Complex Sentences

Transition Words	Punctuation
And	:
But	;
Or	-
However	. . .
Therefore	,
Thus	( )
As a result	
Moreover	
In addition to	
Nevertheless	

makes sense

Again, many of these can be posted in the classroom regardless of what you teach. It sets an expectation of writing quality to see, hanging around the room, posters that are not just on content information, but on methods to communicate that content as well.

how can I incorporate?

Cloze Paragraphs

Another scaffold you can provide are cloze paragraphs to help structure overall writing. These are like fill-in blank paragraphs, like MadLibs, remember? It's a simple strategy, but one that many secondary teachers don't use because there is an assumption that students should somehow write at a certain level before they hit sixth or even ninth grade. *True - which is I'm slowing down in 6th*

True, they should. But when we are setting up expectations of writing standards in classes that aren't English, it's wise to rewind a little and remind students of your level of expectations in communicating the subject matter in your class. Remind them that good writing and solid structure is not to be tapped only in their English class.

Figure 7.8 is an example of a cloze paragraph for a scientific argument.

This activity is not meant to substitute for their own writing, but really serves a purpose in creating a standard of writing regardless of your content.

TTW—Think, Talk, Write

The TTW strategy, Think, Talk, Write, is a strategy I originally learned from the California Writing Project. For secondary students, this strategy is vital. Writing is about communicating ideas that are in one's head. But with teenagers especially, brainstorming and discussion is key in honing in on the highest-level (or appropriate) ideas on which to write.

Have students use TTW by having them work with partners. Working with partners and reading/talking about what we are learning or what they have written about helps students retain information and helps them learn how to get better in communicating their knowledge.

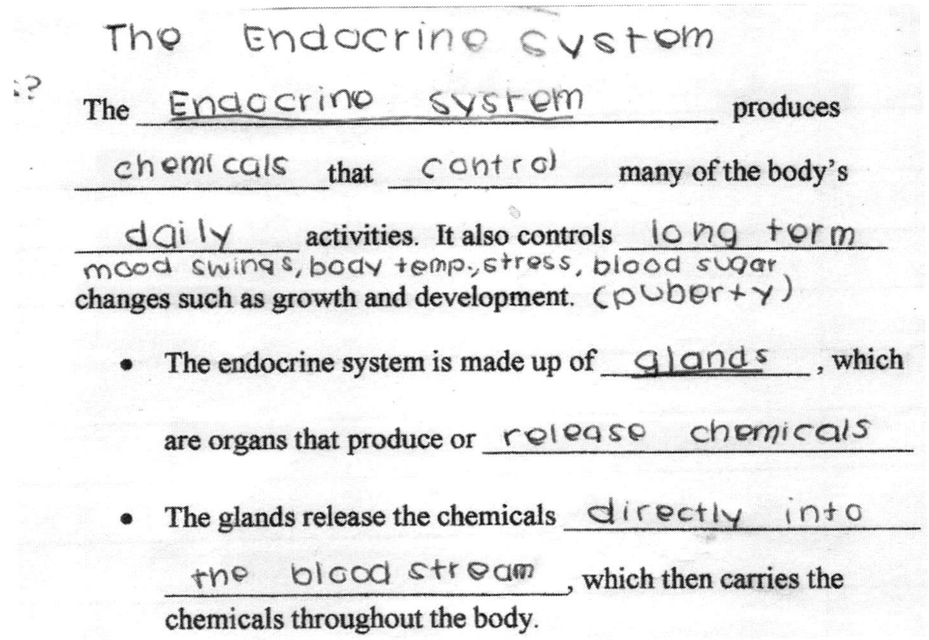

The Endocrine System

:?

The ___Endocrine System___ produces

___chemicals___ that ___control___ many of the body's

___daily___ activities. It also controls ___long term___
mood swings, body temp., stress, blood sugar
changes such as growth and development. (puberty)

- The endocrine system is made up of ___glands___, which

  are organs that produce or ___release chemicals___

- The glands release the chemicals ___directly into___

  ___the blood stream___, which then carries the

  chemicals throughout the body.

FIGURE 7.8

Educator and author Sheridan Blau once said, "Reading is a social activity that needs to happen in conversation." The same can be said for writing. Allow students time to think about the topic at hand. Allow them to discuss their thoughts. Then give them the opportunity to write. It is a way to permit collaboration while still keeping individuals accountable. It's also more engaging for them, and will produce a higher level of writing for you.

Having said that, however, collaboration shouldn't just end in the brainstorming and idea-formulating chapter of an assignment. In fact, you should train them not only to discuss, but also to teach each other.

Train Them to Be Teachers

As I've written about in the past, when you look at a writing rubric in my classroom, you'll notice that "Able to Teach" (A2T) is the highest evaluation a student can receive. For a student to get an A2T score, he or she must show, through their writing, that they understand the content so well that they could teach it to others.

Throughout the year, I train them to be able to be teachers in many ways. There are specific methods, however, that focus only on the writing process, and once I teach students what I want from them, I can let go a little bit with being the authority in the room, trusting the students to do much of what I do as a writing coach and mentor. This allows me time and energy to focus on content and on differentiating with students who need it the most.

The two strategies that I find the most valuable in creating peer writing teachers are peer reviewing and using student-created rubrics (see Chapter 1) in order to have students score each other's writing quality. These scores provide feedback in an efficient way and in a way that many respond to in a deeper way because the advice came from a peer.

If you train students to give feedback to each other, you can focus more on content while the students focus on writing quality. You split the responsibility in a way. And with this split comes ownership of the product and, as a consequence, ownership of the level in which they communicate your content. It's a win–win.

- Peer reviewing—For peer reviewing, I provide a packet of activities to look for when students need to give feedback to their colleagues in their writing quality. Each student is given a piece of writing from another student and does the activities, thus informing the student of what the writing still needs before it can be called a final draft. See Appendix I for a peer review packet dedicated to an argumentation selection that can be used for any content area.

- Peer scoring and student-created rubrics—I have written in the past of the importance of using student-created rubrics in the classroom. Rubrics are key, but it's the additional step of asking students to translate rubrics into their own words that really adds value to their use. In my previous book I look at the process of creating a student-created rubric. In a nutshell, however, once a student analyzes the teacher-ese version of a writing rubric, say for an analysis of some kind, then the student can translate those expectations into their own words. This makes for no confusion about the standards, and ups the ownership of the writing. Use rubrics to set expectations. Don't only show students the rubric at the end of their writing process; show it to them before they write and the writing will be better in the end. (See Appendix B for an example of a student-created rubric that one of my periods created collaboratively.)

Teaching Academic Vocabulary

So this isn't a strategy per se, but I'm including it here because writing isn't just about structure, it's also about word choice. There are different strategies for incorporating and actively teaching academic vocabulary in any classroom. Full disclaimer: I'm not a big fan of the weekly vocabulary quiz. It's a drill-and-kill strategy that I fear does not transfer between classes or outside of school. However, there are strategies that help embed vocabulary further. I will share two here.

- Word window—the word window appeals to different modalities of students. That is, it asks for students to interact with the vocabulary in different ways and, in so doing, embeds the words further. Here is a template for a word window. Once a student has seen it, he or she can recreate this template into their writer's notebook so you don't have to waste paper. Figure 7.9 is an example of a word window created using a math term, and Figure 7.10 shows a word window using a historical term. Figure 7.11 shows one that uses a term typical of academic vocabulary.

FIGURE 7.9

- Pre-assessment—If you do plan on administering vocabulary quizzes, I would consider some kind of pre-assessment in order for students to get their hands dirty a little with the words first. I always liked this pre-assessment inspired by the AVID program used by many. AVID stands for Advancement Via Individual Determination, and their strategies can help with writing, literacy, study skills, and college readiness. In this pre-assessment, students first write down the words they will be tested on. They then evaluate their prior knowledge of the word. Check it out in Table 7.3.

Using Acronyms

Acronyms are not just for elementary levels. Secondary students use them to remember higher-level expectations. Once taught, students can accesses these terms easily rather than asking you, "What do we do next?" In terms of writing,

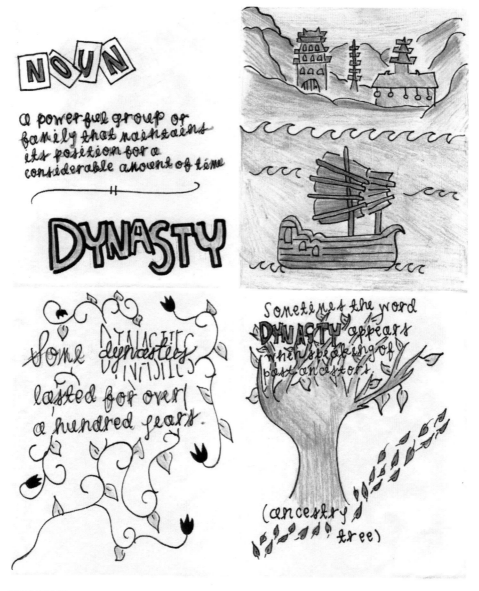

FIGURE 7.10

there are many that are worth noting, but I wanted to share with you a couple in particular that all classes could use to remember the process of writing.

- P.O.W.E.R.S.—Based on the work by Carl Young, this acronym stands for Pre-writing, Organize, Write, Edit, Revise, and Share. Some strategies for each may include, but are not limited to:
  - Pre-writing—Using a writing notebook, think, talk, write, webbing, graphic organizers, quickwrites, quickdraws, observing and reflecting, etc.

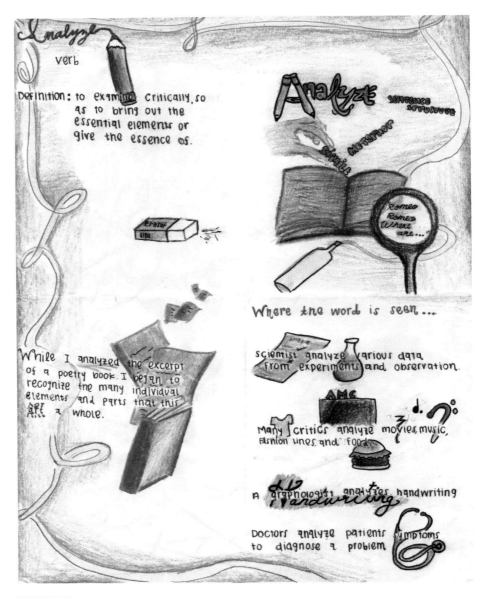

FIGURE 7.11

- Organizing—Outlining, clustering, numbering in sequence, answering the 5Ws of writing (who, what, when, where, why).
- Write.
- Editing—Using a checklist, reading your rough draft backwards to evaluate one's own writing out of context, recording and listening to one's own writing, filling out peer rubrics, using correct conventions, etc.

TABLE 7.3 Sample Vocabulary Pre-Assessment

Word	Could Teach It	Sounds Familiar	Have No Idea
Pythagorean Theorem		X	

- Revising—Using the STAR acronym created by Kelly Gallagher to help students remember different ways they can revise (Substitute, Take Things Out, Add, and Rearrange). Use the CPR strategy (listed earlier) to add commentary.
- Share—Presenting the writing to a peer or group of peers provides a vital audience for a final draft. Even if an assignment is just passed to the person on their right, it still has power to share one's efforts with those who will appreciate them.

Creating Flipbooks

Earlier in this book I mentioned storyboarding (see Chapter 4). Flipbooks are a different format of these in that they focus on sequential information or information categorized by topics. In addition, they add a tactile modality to a lesson since the student must fold and staple to create the flipbook they will be filling.

A typical flipbook uses additional modalities as well, in that it combines pictures, created by the student, as well as text.

In terms of what disciplines can use this strategy, the answer is all. Think about it: a history class might use it to help a student understand the branches of government. A science class might use it to help a student communicate the steps of an experiment. An ELA teacher might use it to summarize a novel by chapters. A math teacher might use it to explain different equations and how they apply in the world beyond.

Darlene Pope, history teacher extraordinaire, literacy coach and trainer for both the College Board and AVID, uses flipbooks for all of her students. She understands that the rigor of history can be supported by writing, and asks her students to produce flipbooks to capture their thoughts on particular eras or topics. She uses flipbooks as a pre-writing assessment of content for students to use before jumping into more traditional essay writing. From the pictures below of both the closed flipbooks and open flipbooks, you can see how explicit the details are in terms of supporting the ideas and evidence necessary for the next step in the writing process. Of course, you can also use flipbooks to be your culminating writing assessment as well; it all depends on how you define your parameters. Figures 7.12 through

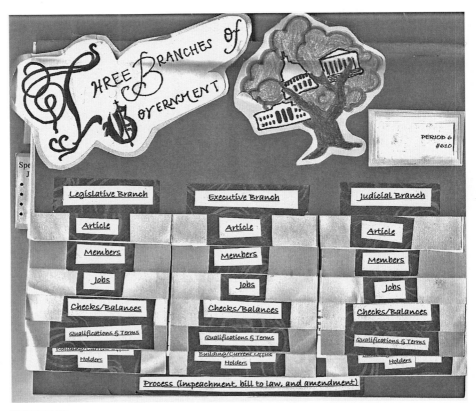

FIGURE 7.12

7.15 show pictures of student-created pre-assessment flipbooks from Pope's class that focus on history. You'll notice that Figure 7.14 also ends on a summary page.

Each page uses a picture and/or symbols, and combines that with a summary of the concept. It can also include some textual evidence, perhaps a quote from the textbook or a primary document to add an even deeper level to the information being presented.

To create a real simple version of a flipbook, check out this digital resource from ReadWriteThink: www.readwritethink.org/files/resources/interactives/flipbook.

Providing a Classroom Library

It doesn't matter if you teach science, math, history, Spanish, or woodshop. You should still have a classroom library.

As I have said in the past in my book *'Tween Crayons and Curfews: Tips for Middle School Teachers*,

> I believe a classroom library is the heartbeat of a teacher's environment. It is the window into their own personality [and] it reflects the importance of

FIGURE 7.13

literacy in the classroom . . . For one thing, having a great library promotes student achievement, and for another, it introduces the students to what you love, and that knowledge of you, and that possible connection to them, makes teaching easier.

FIGURE 7.14

The best silver bullet (OK, even better than blogging) in helping students learn to write is in providing access to the kind of writing you want them to see. This means creating a corner of your room in which students can explore the great writers of your content. You don't have to have an eclectic mix of genres in your library to provide a valuable classroom resource. Begin to develop a classroom library that is filled with examples, both literary and nonfiction, which help illuminate your content. Gather picture books, comic books, graphic novels, young adult novels, classics, poetry, nonfiction, etc. Bring in a daily newspaper and subscribe to student friendly periodicals in your subject matter. Encourage them to read whatever strikes their fancy even if it seems that it is not challenging them. Once you get them hooked on your library, then you can direct them to more challenging materials.

For instance, let's say you are a PE teacher. Perhaps an area of the fitness lab can be designated for a reading resource corner. Perhaps in it you have a subscription to *Sports Illustrated for Kids*. You also have sports sections of newspapers, biographies of sports legends, young adult fiction by Mike Lupica, or a classic like *Shoeless Joe* (on which *Field of Dreams* was based). The best way to encourage writing is to encourage reading. It provides the model and the excitement to communicate what the students are studying.

The Lincoln-Douglas Debates
Date- 1858
Important People- Stephen Douglas, Abraham Lincoln
Main Points- Douglas wanted country to be half free and half slave while Lincoln wanted one or the other. Lincoln and Douglas held debates over slavery and politics.
Significance- Douglas won election; Lincoln became famous. Brought slavery under limelight.

John Brown's Raid

Lincoln's Election

FIGURE 7.15

There is an integral relationship between reading and writing. By setting up a classroom environment that encourages reading, you will, almost through the process of osmosis, be supporting writing as well.

For a rich plethora of additional strategies on teaching writing, check out these resources:

- *Strategies That Work: Teaching Comprehension for Understanding and Engagement* by Stephanie Harvey and Anne Goudvis.

- *The Reading/Writing Connection: Strategies for Teaching and Learning in the Secondary Classroom* (3rd edition) by Carol Booth Olson.

- *Best Practices in Writing Instruction (Solving Problems in Teaching of Literacy)* by Steve Graham, Charles A. MacArthur, and Jill Fitzgerald.

- *Scaffolded Writing Instruction: Teaching with a Gradual-Release Framework (Teaching Strategies)* by Douglas Fisher and Nancy Frey.

Writing with Technology
for the Common Core

> Students who are college and career ready . . . use technology and digital media strategically and capably . . . Students employ technology thoughtfully to enhance their reading, writing, speaking, listening, and language use. They tailor their searches online to acquire useful information efficiently, and they integrate what they learn using technology with what they learn offline. They are familiar with the strengths and limitations of various technological tools and mediums and can select and use those best suited to their communication goals.
>
> (Common Core State Standards Initiative)

There is a vital relationship between Common Core and technology in a way there has not been with previous standards and assessments. These appropriate bedfellows are now driving both the methods of teaching and the methods of testing; and I admit I am intrigued where it will take us as an educational system.

As they currently stand, the Common Core online assessments will be a combination of both an online multiple-choice test and some kind of performance-based assessment, be it a traditional written essay or a more visually embedded project of sorts uploaded into a field for scoring.

There are pros and cons to the system, but this doesn't mean that there are pros and cons to the intention or the outcome.

Many fear that the assessments are just another bubble test with students clicking rather than bubbling. They make a good argument here. After all, if the level of content doesn't reflect more real-world applications or higher-level thinking then what's the difference?

Many also fear that schools are not prepared for technology to play a larger daily role in education. If students are being assessed with the assumption that they are comfortable with technology, that means that students must be using technology not just to be assessed. Are schools prepared? Are teachers trained and using it daily? Is there enough equipment?

However, I would argue that while it's true the content must reflect higher levels for our students, the act of using technology is heading our students in the right direction. Clicking items, managing fields, uploading work, these are all skills our students need to be able to do. According to the white paper written by Lauren Davis, "5 Things Every Teacher Should be Doing to Meet the Common Core

Standards," the Common Core assessments ask for a greater "focus on procedure, not just content."

Assessing wags the dog, as we've said, and with these skills being tested will undoubtedly come a higher level of integration of some of these real-world skills in the classroom. In fact, history teacher Rod Powell says, "I think the digital literacy that a student develops from immersion in a digital classroom carries over into the workplace."

From his standpoint, and many others, classrooms will surely benefit from the philosophical move from technology as recommended to technology as required. After all, as Gary Stager, founder of Constructing Modern Knowledge, states in this "Q & A with Larry Ferlazzo":

> The personal computer is used to amplify human potential. It is an intellectual laboratory and vehicle for self-expression that allows each child to not only learn what we've always taught, perhaps with greater efficacy, efficiency or comprehension . . . This vision of computing democratizes educational opportunity and supports what Papert and Turkle call epistemological pluralism. The learner is at the center of the educational experience and learns in their own way.

In other words, if we are differentiating, individualizing, and making more applicable our educational system, then technology must be utilized in a more integrated way than in the past.

However, teachers are also concerned that students need training in all the skills that they will need just to participate in the test. Teachers are nervous about the amount of instructional time needed to ensure that students are ready for the tests.

I respectfully disagree with this concern. I predict students will manage quite nicely. It's the adjustment in classroom teaching that will have a metamorphosis as a result of the Common Core assessment plan. Students are flexible. They will learn. The third grade student who struggles to upload the first year of the testing implementation will surely be prepared in how to upload by the time they are in sixth grade. The student who first takes the assessments during his or her sixth grade year will undoubtedly know how to do so more smoothly by seventh grade. I anticipate some bumps in students' tech knowledge, but these will be short-lived as the tests become more and more used with every year.

Furthermore, I think that clicking a bubble is far more intuitive and simple to accomplish than nearly bubbling a circle with a #2 pencil.

I once did an experiment along these lines. During a standardized reading test for my district, I asked my students to circle the correct letter in the reading packet before bubbling the same letter onto the Scantron sheet. When the results came back, I asked the students to look at the letter they intended to bubble and the letter that they actually bubbled. There were countless errors, not because the students did not understand the content, but because the bubbling was, believe it or not, a skill at which not all students succeed 100 percent of the time. In fact, one eighth grade honors student I had made six bubbling errors alone on a fifty-point test! My point is that bubbling is a more difficult fine-motor skills issue than

really! [handwritten annotation in left margin]

clicking. I'm not saying that clicking is foolproof, but it will hopefully set more students up for success because it is asking them to communicate in a simpler and more familiar way.

Many fear that a computer-scored writing process cannot reward student effort and creativity. How do we score writing if humans are not the ones scoring it? Teachers are concerned that in an attempt to be equitable, we are sacrificing creativity. That was, after all, the flaw of a standardized system. How do we avoid this?

Today's technologies are rich with assessment opportunities. However, the teaching philosophies of yore, at times, are at odds with the potential. As an example, take MyAccess, an online writing assessment program that scores and gives feedback using a simple rubric at the click of the submit button. Many K12 schools use MyAccess, but it unfortunately is not keeping up with the 4Cs—creativity, critical thinking, collaboration, and communication—in that it only recognizes foundational writing skills and not voice, creative sentence fluency, ideas, organization (beyond the traditional five paragraph structure), or word choice. These five out of six traits that are recognized as a means to teach writing allow for both traditional writers and those who think out of the box. MyAccess, however, does not allow for both. In fact, it scores towards the lowest common denominator, as many standardized systems do.

MyAccess reminds me of a musical experiment that was conducted years ago. A record company decided to study the most popular songs and analyze their components; they then had a computer write a new song fitting those components together using a sort of perfect pop song equation. What they ended up with was blah. No personality. No voice. No uniqueness. MyAccess is much the same. As an assessment program, it doesn't recognize anything beyond its standardized rubric as correct. Thus, it helps to train students in writing . . . well . . . blah.

Nevertheless, while I was fearful of this too, I have become more relaxed about the technology involved. According to Erik Robelen's article in *Education Week*, "Man vs. Computer: Who Wins the Essay-Scoring Challenge?" a study was conducted in which essays were scored by both. The results were astoundingly similar. Now, this means one of two things: either computer scoring technology has gotten better over the years (it has, after all, been used to score countless essays in higher education) by recognizing quality despite variety, or teachers themselves don't score creatively or critically. I prefer to think the former.

Despite the concerns, however, the requirement of these assessments will undoubtedly drive innovation. For one thing, the multiple-choice portion of the assessment created by the SMARTER consortium will be adaptive. That's already an improvement on the tests of yore. That is, they will adjust based on the level of the participant.

Ever take a Facebook quiz? You know, the ones that ask, "What species in Middle Earth are you?" or "What character in *Downton Abbey* are you?" Well, the computer adaptive testing (CAT) section works like that. Rather than the test being linear, it's more like a complex flow chart. What you answer for one question determines the question that you will get next. It's a differentiated assessment. We're heading in the right direction.

Clearly we have to be careful about technology's use in this next educational generation. Computers, after all, cannot replace a great teacher; and even a test that is administered online is not necessarily a good assessment if its content is weak. Therefore, the method of testing online alone is not enough to justify its use.

However, I do believe that, by incorporating technology in a more determined way, it will bring education one step closer in preparing our students for their future.

If the assessments ask students to collaborate, to brainstorm, and to write, then hopefully more and more interdisciplinary classes will too. To meet this new age, perhaps more teachers will ask students to participate in online asynchronous discussions. Maybe more teachers will ask students to create collaborative wikis or blog with one another in content-area clubs. Maybe more teachers will ask students to use graphic organizers to brainstorm or use apps like ShowMe to help them post their knowledge online.

Technology allows us to do those things . . . if the instructor asks it.

Modeling to Create a Tech-Rich Classroom

Many classrooms out there already have access to a certain degree of technology. Many classrooms, however, still do not; and the technological expectations can be daunting. Nevertheless, there are easy things that can be done in any classroom, regardless of the teacher's comfort with technology, embracing tech in a way that trickles down to a hesitant learner and addresses the Common Core.

In this section, I don't necessarily want to talk about how to "use" technology in the classroom, so much as how to "model" technology. After all, I believe that the students who are most comfortable with educational technology are those that are submerged in it, watching their teacher simply use it in their everyday life. And that's the point.

Technology is in our everyday life now. School cannot be divested of it. But this doesn't mean that a student needs a hands-on training in a 1:1 district in order to know how to use a computer come testing time. Many teachers believe that if students aren't actively sitting in front of the computer screen themselves, then clearly technology is not being used in the classroom. I beg to disagree.

This myth can be a gatekeeper of sorts for many teachers, so I wanted to create a list that gives advice on how to use technology through modeling. By simply modeling the use of technology, the students are also learning to use it in an indirect way.

Additionally, these are strategies that can work in any secondary classroom for any subject. And by folding in technology in a more organic way, you are encouraging the 4Cs. After all, using technology is as much about communication as it is about content. It's about critical thinking and problem-solving. It's about creativity as well as collaboration. Modeling technology in the classroom welcomes the student community into your thought process and makes it a less isolated experience.

It's all about Think Aloud, that age-old trick of simply narrating everything you are doing as the wiser, more experienced brain in the room. Narrate your decisions and your rationale and you will be teaching your students how to make good decisions both online and off. Good behavior online is trickle-down, after all. Model it, live it, talk about it.

1. Post a list of norms for online and offline behavior and keep it up. Refer to it. Make it a part of your classroom culture.

2. Make your LCD projector and/or interactive whiteboard a daily part of how you teach lessons.

3. Set up your technology in front of your students while talking them through the process. Eventually, create a "tech crew" made up of first period students that set up your technology during announcements in the morning. Maybe they come in a few minutes early. However you want to work it, ask the students to be involved.

4. No matter if you have a one-computer or a ten-computer classroom, you can have resources available and open at all times using the computer as a station. Can't find the right word when you're modeling writing an informational response? Walk over to the computer while you are talking to the students and use visualthesaurus.com to find just the right word. Keep Visual Thesaurus open during writing assignments so students can follow your lead and use it transparently in front of the class too.

5. Use a document camera for sharing student work.

6. Skype with another teacher on campus in front of the classes. It's a fishbowl strategy of sorts that models video-conferencing norms. Discuss the topic together. Share work in which you have pride. In no time, students will be able to video-conference with each other with similar poise.

7. Take a photo of an interesting location with your cell phone, email it to yourself, and use it the next day to help teach a concept: descriptive writing about a setting, for example. Show students you are thinking of their learning even outside of the classroom. After all, learning shouldn't end at the bell.

8. Be transparent with your Google searches. Use Google Advanced Search while on the LCD projector and use Think Aloud to share why you are using the keywords that you are using.

9. Look at the law on copyright infringement together as a class. Revise some multiple-choice reading comprehension questions to assess their understanding of this vital informational text. *Voilà!* Informational test prep that applies to the real world!

10. Present your lesson using a PowerPoint or a Prezi. Better yet, initially create it with input from the class so they can see how you assemble it. Now you're discussing content and methodology.

11. Show an excerpt from a TED.com video to introduce a concept. Model how to navigate through the menus to find just the right video with the topic you seek.

12. Use your interactive whiteboard in any way that you know how. Even if you don't have it all under your belt just yet, use Think Aloud to babble about how to open files, save files, change colors and fonts, create slides, create a link, etc., as you move through your subject–matter lesson.

13. Allow students to see how you organize your computer desktop. For any document you seek to open, make your search transparent so that they understand more and more the concept of file organization.

14. Rather than having some photos of your own family stuck with magnets on your mini-fridge door, use a digital frame on your desk with scrolling pictures from your own collection. It just adds to the ambiance of a 21st century environment, which is the habitat in which the students live outside of school's walls.

15. Model reflection by keeping a transparent blog related to your classroom's activities so that people know what's going on. Perhaps it's as simple as a sentence or two that sums up a lesson, but help students realize that thinking back embeds the lesson even further.

16. Set up an email contact list of your students (if the student is old enough, help them set up a Gmail account if they don't have an email account already). Send out a blast of a cool resource or two every now and then. Let them know when there's an interesting local museum exhibit or book signing. Send them a resource for a research paper they may not have heard of. Model how to use email.

17. Use an excerpt from a class at iTunes U to help enhance a lesson or concept. Model how to navigate the site.

18. Download Evernote to all of your devices so that as anything occurs to you (questions, eureka moments, resources discussed, etc.) you can whip out your smartphone, laptop, iPad, whatever, and model using the Cloud for ongoing note-taking.

19. Use technology in your offline vocabulary. Refer to "files" when talking about organizing different classroom resources. Ask students to share by also occasionally calling it "uploading" for the class. Use words like "collaboration" and "networks" when working in small groups. These are not just techno-logical terms, they are 21st century terms, and should be embedded into your teaching.

20. Model flexibility. Remember, whenever you use technology, things go wrong. Have a Plan B or at least model "water off a duck." It will be the most important lesson you can model because life, both online and off, requires us to shrug sometimes and simply move on.

Digital Learning Tips for Students

As an educator, I have definitely evolved from tech tentative to tech tenacious in a very short period of time. Because of my recently found passion for educational technology, I want to share some of the scaffolds I've developed to help my students evolve into digital learners.

In order to help them prep for an eventual transition to web-facilitated (some online usage) or hybrid schooling (up to 80 percent online), I've been pulling together a list of qualities common to many successful online learners. As many of us incorporate more and more online lessons, written assignments, assessments, and digital presentations into our instruction, it's important for students to understand the skills that they will need to function at their best.

The good news is that succeeding in an online environment isn't so different than succeeding in a traditional classroom. OK, sure, there's the time and distance and technological wall that can separate online learners. But the computer, in many cases, doesn't slam the communication door closed; it in fact opens it wider.

But it's good to know what you're getting into. So to help teachers communicate their expectations to students who are just starting to blog or use Dropbox or set up discussion threads, I've provided a list of characteristics that many agree successful distance learners possess. Notice the similarities in many of the attributes that our students need to succeed in a traditional classroom. The difference, of course, is that one's success relies far more on individual choices and energy management. Here are seven attributes students should have or need to develop for successful online learning:

1. **You have to have a sense of self.** Successful learners online have an awareness of metacognition—self-motivation, self-starting, and ownership of one's actions. In other words, they reflect on how they learn as well as what they learn.

2. **You need to be able to manage your time wisely.** They must be able to lay out their tasks with a critical eye, plan them accordingly, and follow them through to fruition—many times without someone looking over their shoulder.

3. **You have *got* to know how to collaborate.** This is a biggie. More than an understanding of technology, more than a perfection of writing skills, the ability to collaborate is one that must be used comfortably online.

4. **You need to be able to set goals for yourself.** Being able to see the target and backwards plan towards that target is vital.

5. **You need to communicate well in writing.** The entire online community is based on the language of words and how to communicate them effectively. One cannot use texting language and expect to be heard. A student needs to use their best level of writing.

6. **You must follow the community norms.** Just like a classroom has a set of rules, so does an online class. A student must function within the norms and rules of netiquette set up by the instructor (or, better yet, agreed upon by the class itself).

7. **You must be your own advocate.** As slam poet Taylor Mali once wrote when asked if they would be tested on the material, "If not you, then who?" So does it go with being one's own advocate. If you won't ask the questions, take control, and make sure your voice is heard in a positive way . . . then who will?

Still not convinced that online learning is similar to your traditional classroom? Well, as I wrote about in my last book, business leaders and college professors have identified thirteen skills as those most needed by students entering college or the workforce. Just to recap, they are as follows:

> Collaboration, Independent Learning, Communication, Problem Solving, Decision Making, Understanding Bias, Leadership, Questioning, Persuasion, Goal-Setting, Sharing the Air, Compromise, Summarizing.

Clearly all of these skills are interrelated and weave together in some form or another. But now look at the seven skills of distance learners above. See any similarities? Online learning contributes to one's education of both college and career readiness, and that's the goal. Use this list as a sort of rubric. Let the students know of your expectations online and I bet you'll see that door begin to swing steadily more open.

The Common Core world is one that enthusiastically embraces technology. Many of our schools, however, are not prepared for that world. Yet sometimes in education, the system only moves as quickly as the demands upon it. Although many have been yelling for more technology or more innovative means to assess students, the glacial movement towards that goal has been frustrating. With the Common Core era, however, we've had to ramp up technologies in schools, and I'm of the belief that it was a needed kick in the pants.

I do have disappointment, however, that these new standards have not come with the advice or the budget to fill holes in the existing technologies in many schools. However, I would argue that these holes will be filled because they have to be. In the past, many boards of education and state departments of education pooh-poohed the surge towards educational technology, leaving much to the efforts and pockets of individual teachers and schools. Unfortunately, this has left a gap in many schools' ability to use technology. With the Common Core movement, the decision to invest in our children's future and the decision to invest in educational technology has been taken off the table of "Maybe later" and brought to the forefront of "How do we make this happen?" So to many, this relationship between Common Core and technology is a blessing for the system as a whole.

It is vital to invest in the future, even a little, even while budgets are being slashed in the present. We are, after all, in the business of preparing people for the future.

What Kind of Tech-Savvy Teacher Do You Want To Be?

At this point, some of you might be ready to jump even further into utilizing educational technology. Perhaps you're ready to move beyond modeling technology and into a more blended percentage of instruction, incorporating both online and offline strategies. I bring this up because the key, most often used method of communicating when online is to write. Students can't avoid it. So if your dedication to integrating writing is propelling you forward into a more writing-dominated environment, perhaps blended learning is for you. But know it isn't an easy road and it isn't a silver bullet. What it is, however, is a domino effect that will change your classroom practice forever . . . and for the better.

Online classes are at a crossroads. They can go the way of correspondence courses: "look at this, then submit" as so many of the iTunes U classes are set up to be. They can also redefine what we think about education and methodology.

All eyes are focused on what kind of education online classes will become. But it is a supply-and-demand market. Will online programs continue down the road of "sage on the stage" with their Massive Open Online Course (MOOC) model, or will they adopt the more effective and more innovating "guide on the side" model that many of us know to be the better way to teach?

Unfortunately, many of those who are involved with the future of online education remain mired in the tired strategies still seen in many of our best colleges and universities. Massive classes, no teacher contact, isolated learning in a room of many. Formative assessments may be implemented, but they aren't informal or multi-modal. Summative assessments are multiple-choice or a standard written essay based on lecture, note-taking, or viewing with very little collaboration involved. This is not teaching, and I daresay it is also not the deepest learning.

So while we have the technology to enrich the teaching and learning process, we are still in transition as people learn a more active and dynamic way to relay and assess information. When it comes to successful online learning, today's technology allows for synchronous discussions, asynchronous conversations, and collaboration in real time and at each learner's convenience. Today's technologies allow for not only the chance to assess one's knowledge but, arguably more importantly, a person's ability to communicate that knowledge in the way that fits more effectively with that person's abilities.

As a K12 classroom teacher, you have a choice. As you begin to entertain adopting more online strategies, you could go down one or the other of the paths listed above. You could use an online classroom simply as a place to store videos of your lectures, posting them for students to view, and asking them to answer a prompt or two for an assignment. You could also use an online classroom to do any of the following and more:

- Set up small student-driven groups to design a website to communicate their content. Have them set evening meetings using Skype or Google Hangout to design a Weebly website with live links to additional research and images to show off the information learned.

- Have students create a collaborative project using Google SketchUp or Photoshop, each adding a new layer and complete with annotations to illustrate a concept.

- Meet online for test prep using something like Blackboard Collaborate. Have students each submit a PowerPoint slide on a content-related term or concept. These slides can then be combined, each contributing to the overall presentation, As each slide comes up, pass the virtual microphone and have that student teach the room about that term.

- Have the students brainstorm as a means to pre-write. Have them use Inspiration to create a web of knowledge, a timeline, or an outline to display their subject matter expertise. Then, have them submit that via a discussion thread to have students give feedback prior to writing a formal draft.

Technology allows us to do those things . . . if the instructor or the program asks it. But instructors and their institutions are slow to hop on the 21st century assessment train. Many teachers don't know how to moderate online discussions, which requires a slightly different skill set than leading one in the classroom. In fact, many online teachers still don't encourage discussion or communication between learners at all, and this gets in the way of advancing the system overall.

Sigh.

What is true, however, is that great online teaching, while different in many ways to one's classroom practice, also reflects great face-to-face teaching. We know, for instance, that class size still matters. The smaller the cohort, the more attention a teacher can give; and we know this aids in achievement. No-brainer. We also know that when a teacher is available after hours to answer questions, it's stunning how many students will be asking questions; thus proving that 3:00 should not be when learning ends. School must be given the resources to continue after the bell rings.

Be prepared, however. Once you open your virtual door after hours, there is an expectation of immediate response and guidance for much longer periods of time than from a traditional classroom teacher. However, the students will pay you back by utilizing that time and being more present than ever before.

Also, while educators know that the smaller the cohort, the more effective the learning, many districts and companies believe that they can save money by loading more learners in with a single instructor. This affects assessments in that it then becomes a challenge to assess in any personalized way.

Programs like Haiku Learning allow you to create an inexpensive online shell in which to house discussions, resources, submissions, videos, and links. For instance, I created an online class for students to introduce them to the concepts of online learning. Figure 8.1 is a screen shot of the expanded menu bar.

Creating an Online Student Lounge

So I hear you've been mulling over building a virtual classroom to weave in some online strategies with your face-to-face traditional classroom. Bravo. You rock. You won't regret it.

The first thing to think about is the purpose of what you wish to accomplish. Are you merely looking for a place to house videos of yourself teaching lessons so students can watch them for review? Or (and I hope this is your answer) are you instead looking for an additional place to build the community of learners? One that could still house lessons, but also can become a place for discussion, informal assessments, and collaboration?

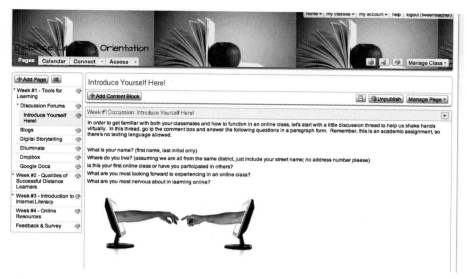

FIGURE 8.1

Let's assume for a second that you want the latter. That being the case, there are many free options to choose from when creating an online classroom. All of them are intuitive and all of them are education-centered.

The program I generally use is Haiku Learning. I've tried Edmodo and my district has My Big Campus, both of which are great; you won't hear me dissing either. But I just tend to like the look and the ease of Haiku overall, so I use that when I can.

Now, as a classroom teacher, on Haiku, you can house up to five different classrooms for free, each with different rosters of students. For instance, in the past I've designed a four-week course for students to help introduce them to online learning tools and expectations prior to taking a full online course. It's a boot camp of sorts that's meant to even the field a bit. I've also designed a daylong course for teachers in differentiation. But perhaps most of you out there don't want to design a whole course, per se. You just want to supplement the classroom so that learning happens outside of school time. Perfect use for an online classroom.

The first thing I would do, however, is provide a place in which your online community can hang out, a student union kind of place.

It is not hard to create a virtual student lounge in an online classroom. Think about what a student union provides and go from there. Make sure that students go there first, familiarize themselves with the space, and are encouraged to return to it time and again to recharge their social batteries.

It should be a place where everyone can hang out and share, posting, uploading and downloading. You can also create a "water cooler" thread of some kind that serves as just a fun way to build your community, introducing students to each other as members of a virtual learning community (VLC). It's important to re-introduce students to each other online even if you are a classroom teacher. Students have an interesting way of sharing online fascinating facts about themselves and their thoughts about lessons in a way that sometimes doesn't come out in the traditional classroom.

There are some elements to think about when setting up the student lounge of your online classroom. For instance, you might want to set up a space or thread . . .

- That allows students to post a picture of themselves, perhaps an avatar or symbol that represents them.
- In which you can post engaging prompts on a regular basis that students can respond to. Make sure the posts are just plain fun.
- Where students can also post their own questions.
- That links to resources or even a gift shop of materials and supplies that students can buy in order to supplement their own learning.
- Where students can share thoughts, writings, and videos.
- That has an "information desk" so students can ask questions about the classroom and/or the content.
- That acts as an "arcade" of links to content-related games and entertainment.
- That promotes and celebrates the learners in the community for their academic or personal accomplishments both online and offline.
- That promotes independent learning by allowing students to ask content-related questions for peers to answer online before coming to you in the traditional classroom the next day. See if students can answer first before being the information authority yourself.

Ensure that your student lounge is comfortable and reflects different modalities in its activities and resources. Make sure it isn't solely text-driven. It should include videos, images, places to discuss, areas to upload so that participants can own some of the content.

Ready to start? Check out some of the resources in the following section. Explore and create the online classroom you think would best supplement your traditional practice, but remember to start with the student lounge.

To help along these lines, I've devoted the remainder of this chapter to a compilation of educational technology resources, broken down into categories. Some of them are from this book but compiled in a more easily accessible way. Others are resources I would simply recommend that have not found mention earlier.

The Big List of Common Core Technology Resources

Creating a student lounge/classroom

- https://www.coursesites.com
- Haiku Learning (www.haikulearning.com)
- www.nicenet.org
- Google Blogger.

Rubric creator

- RubiStar (http://rubistar.4teachers.org).

Graphic organizers for pre-writing activities

- ReadWriteThink (www.readwritethink.org).

Websites that allow students to upload writing, scoring them on the spot

- ETS Criterion (paid service) (www.ets.org/criterion/about?WT.ac=criterion_22703_k12_about_120819)
- Glencoe Online Essay Grader (paid).

Sites on which to publish student work

- Miss Literati (www.missliterati.com/ml/home)
- Lulu (www.lulu.com)
- Mixbook (www.mixbook.com/edu).

Collaboration technology

- WeVideo (www.wevideo.com)
- Dropbox (www.dropbox.com)
- Google Drive (https://drive.google.com).

Real-world applications

- California CareerZone—career finder (www.cacareerzone.org)
- "Why I Write"—Interdisciplinary articles of real-world writing (www.nwp.org).

Interdisciplinary models to use in any class

- TED (www.ted.com)
- Radiolab (www.radiolab.org).

Ways to visualize data

- Google Motion Charts
- Infogr.am (http://infogr.am)
- Piktochart.com (http://piktochart.com)
- Wordle—creates word clouds (www.wordle.com).

Websites that help develop computer-adaptive testing assessments

- www.quiztron.com
- www.quiblow.com
- www.gotoquiz.com.

Sharing work sites or apps

- ShowMe (www.showme.com)
- Educreations (www.educreations.com)
- Screencast (www.screencast.com).

Great professional development resources

- Powerful Learning Practice (http://plpnetwork.com)
- The Infinite Thinking Machine (http://www.youtube.com/user/inifinite thinking)
- Teaching Channel (https://www.teachingchannel.org)
- Edutopia (www.edutopia.org).

Search engines

- Dogpile (www.dogpile.com).

Bookmarking sites

- CiteULike (www.citeulike.org)
- Diigo (https://www.diigo.com)
- Delicious (https://delicious.com).

Blogging sites

- Kidblog (http://kidblog.org/home)
- WordPress (http://wordpress.org)
- Google Blogger (www.blogger.com).

DIY websites

- Weebly (www.weebly.com)
- Google Sites (www.google.com).

DIY apps

- ibuildapp.com.

21st Century Professional Development in Writing for Every Teacher

Teachers became part of professional learning communities, working together, sharing ideas, gathering information, and changing curriculum and instruction in response to what they were learning. Such approaches build school-wide capacity by honoring the knowledge and experience that teachers bring with them.

(Arthur Applebee)

Because writing appears so front-and-center in the Common Core Standards, many are reporting an increase in needed professional development in how to teach and assess writing. After all, assessing writing can be challenging.

When asked why good writing is difficult to assess, Linda Friedrich, PhD, the Director of Research and Evaluation of the National Writing Project, responded that:

The assessment of writing involves a great deal of professional judgment and agreement. Assessment of writing requires a vision for what "good" is—and what constitutes good is layered. It involves content, writing craft, authorial stance, structure, and conventions. In addition, what good is depends on purpose, audience, disciplinary standards, and so on . . . When assessing writing in a school, district, state or other environment, there also needs to be mechanisms for building agreement among those responsible for assessing the writing.

For these reasons, teachers must be permitted time to discuss, plan, and reach consensus.

There are so many resources out there to tell you what you should and shouldn't do to address the Common Core Standards. This book, in fact, can be counted among them. However (and don't tell my publisher I've told you this), I would argue that the best resources out there are you and your school site colleagues.

You are the ones who see those students day in and day out. You are the ones who know what the best practices are to achieve the standards in a way that prepares those students for life beyond school. You are the ones who face the challenges of school life while still striving to achieve the ideal.

Sure, you could hire an outside consultant to help tell you what to do. But why? The fact is that you have the brains right there in your faculty meeting. OK, so not everyone is fully on board with these changes; that's to be expected. We can't wait for 100 percent of any group to be on board with the next chapter of a system's metamorphosis.

Nevertheless, the talent to work on taking your school to the next level is there. The talent to create a universal rubric is there. The talent to design customized outlines for informational short-answer responses is there. The talent to design prompts that incorporate interdisciplinary content scenarios is there. The talent to recognize real-world and authentic possibilities in assessments is there too.

The Common Core Professional Learning Community

To address this, I think that every school site, not just every district, should set up a Common Core Professional Learning Community—a CCPLC, as it were. These groups would meet to discuss the challenges of interdisciplinary common goals. They would think how to move that specific school community towards a higher level of Common Core learning.

I picture Common Core Professional Learning Communities as interdisciplinary groups going forth and creating amazing small academies of projects, assessments, and activities.

Perhaps four teachers across different CORE subjects can ask their students to participate in a related performance-based assessment, one that incorporates writing, and then share the produced artifacts in a gallery walk at a faculty meeting. Perhaps another group of four teachers can create a different written assessment with their students and share out their findings as well. Perhaps the most successful assessments developed can be adopted school-wide. These CCPLCs can:

- Become a cohort that shares resources;
- Design collaborative assessments with common rubrics;
- Compare results and provide data regarding successes and challenges;
- Give each other feedback and share best practices.

Working in cohorts is certainly efficient, but better yet, an entire staff can become a CCPLC. After all, sharing best practices and developing the tools to teach should include the voices of everyone at the table.

So how do we come together and work, not just as individual teachers, but also as a collaborative staff working towards a common goal?

There are many answers to this question, but it all starts with simply setting the train on the track. I believe that to swim laps in the pool of curricular planning, you first need to dip your toe into the water and test everyone's willingness to collaborate.

Find the pioneers eager to be included in the first steps of implementation; fold in additional, newer voices too in the first wave so that you don't only have the same willing teachers who sit on every committee or who say yes to every PD opportunity. You need to have a variety of voices in that first wave in order to model the process for the rest of the staff.

In the next cohort, weave in that next group who don't want to find themselves with a huge learning curve by not involving themselves in the inevitable systemic change happening.

Admittedly, some of this is out of teachers' hands. After all, to do this takes an investment. Administrators and policy makers who help fund programs must find ways to fund the time to allow for collaboration to happen. However, the willingness must be there. The camaraderie must be nurtured and cultivated by those who will benefit the most from the collaboration: the teachers. However, teachers' willingness to collaborate cannot be misunderstood as a willingness to be taken advantage of. So many teachers give of themselves to do what they know is best for the students; however, in the beginning of this movement, teachers must stand together and insist on a different kind of systemic change, one that provides time and resources to plan correctly and deeply.

Of course, collaborating, especially across departments, can be challenging. There are different philosophies and methods of teaching that sometimes pull us in different directions. But with the Common Core world comes a putting aside of differences to exploit our similarities.

The least threatening way to start this process is by focusing on the language that we all share.

Developing a Universal Common Core Language as a Staff

We all need to begin to speak the same language. I'm not talking about sacrificing personal style, but I am talking about consistency in a school site. As a student enters any room in the school, certain vocabulary terms must be echoed throughout the halls of the school. It creates a net, a web as it were, that captures students in academic terms and expectations from which they can't escape.

By developing key terms, it is then possible to jump into the world of common rubrics, simple ways to set expectations and score students so that the web you have created as a staff supports the weight of their thoughts and their assessments.

And let's face it: shared tools are easier to use. Students who see a united message or use united tools in multiple classrooms are more likely to be able to accomplish those universal goals. In this case, if the goal is universal writing, all classes must be on board with a certain level of expectation. This helps with transfer between classes, so that students aren't producing their best for one classroom and yet producing artifacts with questionable quality in others.

Many states have already developed rubrics that districts have adopted as their own. However, I would encourage schools and districts to do their own developing instead, or tweak those already made, to customize the tools for their own demographics and communities. I believe that the more a school site insists on catering to and developing for their own population, the better. You all know your students better than anyone, and the exercise of developing such a rubric is great to have under your belt for your own department's needs.

To develop a universal writing rubric takes a little frontloading. Use this process as a guide for the creation of your own Common Core Common Rubric.

The first thing to do is to identify important and common vocabulary from each department. To create the writing rubric below, I pulled academic vocabulary from the following sources:

- The language from the Common Core Standards for math and English.
- Previously existing rubrics from my school's language arts department. Nobody, after all, wants to reinvent the wheel.
- Previous sections of this book.

So I first compiled a list of keywords from all the writing genres that apply to all disciplines. In other words, I stayed away from words like "figurative language" because they primarily (though not necessarily) apply only to narrative. Instead, I've chosen to focus on the writing standards that are shared by all of the genres and that can be used in every subject. In so doing, the list of academic vocabulary will help inform the creation of a universal rubric that can form a common language for all departments.

To create this list that will serve to seed your common rubric, you can look to writing outlines as well. Examine the structure of a piece of writing coming out of the CORE classes in your school. Look to the outlines that appear in this book or in the classrooms across your own campus and identify the most vital components of each.

From these, I generated the following list:

- Analyze
- Justify
- Argue
- Content
- Evidence.

Using these terms, it then becomes easier to develop a universal rubric that each department can live with. The rubric should serve to help in assigning, creating, and assessing anything from short-answer to long-form essays in any content. That's not to say that they can't be individualized for each teacher's need, but they should each be using a common, recognizable format that all students can bank on. And with consistency comes security; and with security comes comfort; and with comfort come higher levels of work.

The words in the above list, combined with the traditional sentence stems found in the typical writing rubrics found in an English class, then morphed into the rubric in Table 9.1.

Of course, you can always broaden what you are evaluating by keeping it to a rubric based on the 6 Traits (see Chapter 1). Utilizing the words in the above list,

TABLE 9.1 Universal Writing Rubric

	Over and Above	Meets Requirements Goal of Assignment	Does Not Achieve
Content Knowledge	• The author clearly expresses the *content* being assessed.	• The author presents the *content* as learned.	• Based on the information provided in the writing, the author clearly does not understand the concept taught.
	• The author presents *evidence* beyond the textual proof provided by the instructor.	• The author presents *evidence* indicating comprehension of what was provided.	• The writing lacks any *evidence*, original or provided.
	• The author correctly *analyzes* the issue by bringing in original commentary to create a convincing *argument*.	• The author attempts to *analyze* the issue and comprehends the concept by creating an *argument*.	• The author has not *analyzed* the concept and lacks any commentary, thus creating a summary rather than an *argument*.
Writing Quality	• The author has grabbed the reader's attention using a hook.	• The author has a weak, but present, hook.	• There is no hook present.
	• The author includes main topic sentences so that the reader understands what each paragraph will be about.	• The author generally uses main topic sentences.	• The author does not use main topic sentences.
	• The author *justifies* each argument using cited evidence.	• The author attempts to *justify* each argument.	• There is no attempt to *justify* each argument.
	• Correct conventions are used throughout the written product.	• Mostly correct conventions are used throughout the written product.	• The draft is clearly rough and includes many below grade level errors.

but looking through the 6 Traits lens, a very simplistic interdisciplinary rubric might look like the one in Table 9.2.

There are many great resources out there to help generate rubrics. Many of them are free and easy to use. However, of the ones out there, my favorite is RubiStar (http://rubistar.4teachers.org). Check it out for all your rubric-creating needs.

TABLE 9.2 Interdisciplinary Rubric Based on the 6 Traits

	4	3	2	1
Ideas (Content Knowledge)				
Organization				
Conventions				
Voice				
Word Choice				
Sentence Fluency				
Presentation				

Developing Site-Based Training in Writing Across the Disciplines

Once we analyze the standards, we see words like "analyze," "describe," "justify," and "argue" peppered throughout. And these are just in the math standards! When we examine the language, we realize that all teachers will have to assign and assess writing to support their content. Yet how do we ask teachers who don't teach writing or haven't taught it in years to all of a sudden know what to do? What happens if the lack of assessed writing all these years has led to, in a sense, a rigor mortis in teachers' ability to include writing in their curriculum?

The solution is to seek help from others on your school site. The key is to collaborate with others who are already doing the job. That means tapping into the talents of teachers who already teach writing. That's right. The language arts department.

The talent to teach writing is in every department, but I do think your ELA department has, how shall I say, an educational responsibility here, to step up and lend what they know about writing to a school site Common Core Professional Development Community.

Now, if you're an ELA teacher reading this book, don't panic and don't be mad that I just added something to your plate. After all, you signed up as a teacher of literacy and writing; it only makes sense that some of this evolution should fall to you to help guide. On the other hand, if you are a teacher from a different discipline, don't sigh in relief that ELA is taking it on. No way. Nobody gets to get away that easily. Collaboration is just that—working together.

At this point, I want to describe what a possible school site-specific professional development day might look like. Look at the model below. Take what you like. Ditch what you don't. As a school, make it your own.

To aid interdisciplinary teachers in the ability to assign relevant and consistent writing and to assess that writing in a way that is consistent with the lessons being taught in the ELA classroom, there must be a short, meaningful training on each school site combined with ongoing collaborative meetings.

In terms of the follow-up ongoing collaborative meetings, their intent is to give teachers carved-out consistent time to discuss the Common Core challenges more deeply. This requires a commitment from administrators to ensure that this time isn't hijacked by other required discussions on other topics. These periodic pairings, comprised of all teachers on campus, will be more like collaborative duos supporting staff throughout the year with the questions and challenges that come up as schools implement this more broad-based writing program.

It's like creating teacher partner pairs, not as mentor to mentee, but as two mentors coming together to seek a common ground about implementing the Common Core Standards.

This initial training itself should be co-implemented by the school's department chairs in order to bring multiple perspectives to the faculty, and will include the sharing of a universal rubric that all classes can utilize. The purpose of the training is as follows:

1. To allow math teachers an opportunity to analyze the possible structure of a written argumentation.

2. To allow teachers to write model pieces using content from different units they teach throughout the year. By going through the process of writing themselves, they will learn more about how to teach writing skills themselves.

3. To allow teachers a chance to exchange those model pieces with one another in order to walk away with model texts to use for multiple chapters.

4. To train teachers in how to use a rubric by going through the process of scoring their own pieces using a universal rubric. By going through the reflection process themselves, teachers will then be more likely to insist on written reflection from students. The rubric will have been created in advance by teachers and will be used in all subject areas for assessing short argumentation works of writing.

5. To grant interdisciplinary teachers some collaboration time to design prompts in order to walk away with a binder of possible assignments that can be used in the classroom immediately.

6. To pair teachers across the disciplines (or in trios if necessary) in order to continue more specific conversations and collaborative activities between themselves.

After the initial training day in which teachers will walk away with the resources described above as well as the partner pairings, these partners will meet regularly to design, share, evaluate, and reflect on written assessments and writing-based, performance-based assessments.

Six months later, each department should be given release time to get together to share the best practices that were born from the collaboration.

When you are developing your own professional development, make sure that you also give participants an opportunity to give feedback about the process. Use something as simple as SurveyMonkey to provide teachers with a means to share the likes and dislikes about the experience. It's appropriate for two evaluations to be administered, one after the initial one-day training and another six months down the line to gain feedback about the partner pairings process.

Of course, there's bound to be some pushback to assigning and assessing writing, and one can already predict why. For one thing, language arts teachers spend a lot of time grading those papers, and who has time to add writing to their list of products to grade? Well, in anticipation of some of those complaints, I have put together a quick list of tips to help you manage the load.

Quick and Efficient Tips to Score Writing

Some pushback from content-area teachers is that scoring writing takes so much time. Of course, English teachers have long known this to be true, but there are tricks to make it easier and more efficient such that it can no longer be an excuse.

In my last book, I have a whole chapter on this topic that can apply to any subject area. However, in a nutshell, here are a few tips to help transition content-area teachers into content–area writing teachers:

1. Don't use that little red pen to write notes to students. They don't read them. Use rubrics or checklists to save time and highlight feedback quickly.

2. Only look for one skill to assess with each assignment. In other words, if a student has written an essay and you've just discussed the thesis statement, focus your scoring on their thesis statement, not necessarily other elements of that essay.

3. If a student turns in a written assignment, say based on an experiment that was conducted, only focus on a section of writing and look to that one section for indications of writing quality, conventions, and content.

4. Treat written feedback like a scavenger hunt so that they find the mistakes themselves. You can say something like, "In your essay, you have an error in your hypothesis. Find it."

5. Create a key of feedback symbols. Don't bother writing out words. Use abbreviations, teacher texting as it were, to quickly let them know what needs improvement.

6. Train students to be teachers in order to score papers and fill out rubrics as you would. (See Chapter 7 for details on this method.)

7. Use an oral feedback sheet (see Appendix C) so that students take notes on your feedback as you talk to them. After all, they are more likely to embed information if they are doing the work of recording your advice.

8. Stagger due dates. There is no reason why all 250 essays need to come in on the same day. Save yourself and your view of the students over the mountainous piles that would appear otherwise.

And when all those artifacts are scored, then where do they go? How do you share them with your staff? The answer lies online, in a virtual faculty lounge that is meant to not only build community, but also to also build a more Common Core–educated cohort of staff.

Developing an Online Common Core Themed Faculty Lounge

No time for face-to-face collaboration? You can also create a place where staff can "hang out" online. This faculty lounge of sorts can function as an archive of resources for which teachers can gain access when it is convenient for them to do so.

Programs like Haiku Learning allow you to create an inexpensive online shell in which to house discussions, resources, submissions, videos, and links. For instance, I created an online PD module focused on differentiation for my school site. Figure 9.1 is a screen shot of the expanded menu bar.

You can see that it is broken down into different topics, informal assessments, and a summative assessment. It weaves videos, external links, downloadables, and discussion threads all together so that it is hopefully engaging to those who go through the workshop. It was created to be an online resource for teachers on my school site who want a brush-up on the concept of differentiation. It includes videos of advice from teachers to teachers.

> Differentiation 101
> Tour the Platform
> What Exactly is Differentiation?
> ▼ Differentiating Your Classroom Environment
>   Grouping for Differentiation
>   Informal Assessment: Photograph Analysis
> ▼ Learning Styles vs. Multiple Intelligences
>   What's Your Multiple Intelligence?
>   Examples of Differentiated Lessons
> ▼ Differentiating for our Population
>   Response to Intervention
>   Gifted and Talented
>   English Language Learners
>   RSP
>   Informal Assessment: What's Common?
> ▼ Student Choice
>   Creating Independent Learners
>   Student Goal Setting
>   Creating Differentiated Assessments
>   Summative Written Assessment: Differentiating a Standardized Lesson
>   Summative Assessment: Online Survey
> ▼ Conclusion
>   Course Evaluation Survey
>   Certificate Download
>   Access to Your New VLC

FIGURE 9.1

Using this same format, a school site can also develop resources and an online VLC (a virtual learning community) using their own learning management system. Some schools are on Edmodo, some are on My Big Campus. Others might be using Google or Haiku or Blackboard. Regardless, it is not hard to create a virtual lounge area of Common Core information in which all can hang out, learning and sharing, posting, uploading and downloading. You can also create a "water cooler" thread of some kind that serves as just a fun way to build your community.

For the Edutopia Middle School Group I began a thread on "Your favorite teacher movie of all time." With over a hundred comments, it appears to be the go-to place for just a fun read and conversation. Perhaps there are other threads that can entice lurkers out of the corners and help others, with a tendency to leadership, harness some of their contributions into a written online forum.

Just remember, when you develop an online faculty lounge for fellow teachers:

- Make it simple. Ensure that it is accessible to all participants by being sensitive to the different levels of tech savvy on your site. To do this, select an easy-to-use learning management system (LMS).
- Ensure that it reflects different modalities in its activities and resources as you would any unit for any age group. Make sure it isn't solely text-driven. It should include videos, images, places to discuss, areas to upload so that participants can own some of the content. It should also have ways for teachers to ask questions.
- Have it reflect the knowledge of people in all the departments, not just your own. Make sure the voices you record or quote from or video are diverse in what they bring to the table. Make sure they represent all departments.

When developing an online staff resource shell, think metaphorically. What rooms might you want to enter if you were in a huge Common Core university? A possible menu of tabs for a Common Core virtual faculty lounge might be the following:

- Well, I know that I'd want a place for participants to hang out in, a student lounge of sorts where participants can get to know one another or post more personal photos and threads. It should be comfortable and full of entertainment.
- There should be classrooms of different topics, places where visitors can go to explore categorized subjects. Perhaps a math Common Core room, an ELA Common Core room, and rooms where teachers can go to see what other teachers in all the disciplines are doing.
- There should be a gallery of best practices.
- There should be a library, an archive of resources.
- Maybe there is a gift shop, a place where people can purchase or share information and best practices.

Feeling brave enough to jump into creating your faculty's online lounge? There are some great free resources out there for doing so. The following programs all have free options, all are intuitive and easy to use, and are all able to house a variety of needs for your VLC.

- https://www.coursesites.com
- http://www.haikulearning.com
- http://www.odijoo.com/pages/overview/create_online_courses
- http://www.nicenet.org
- http://moodle.com/.

Get Thee to a Writing Project!

As a teacher, you can only do so much to learn about subjects other than those in which you specialize. After that, you have to lean on others to teach you. That's where the National Writing Project comes in.

I chose to end this book with a call to action. I'm hoping, in a way, this book serves as an argument for why it's vital we all incorporate writing and how, when tasked to do so, our writing assessments don't have to limit how we teach our content. Even though writing is now a given in this new Common Core world, it shouldn't limit our content that we love so much. It should help it to bloom.

So my call to action is this: now that you know why you need to integrate writing, get thee to a Writing Project. It is a brain spa for those who feel recharged after dunking themselves into the waters of reflection and learning.

The National Writing Project can help where books, webinars, and blog posts can't. It is devoted to helping teachers learn to write, and, more specifically, learn to teach writing, by giving them access to some of the greatest writing teachers around. Its official mission, according to the NWP website and Dr. Linda Friedrich, the NWP's Director of Research and Evaluation, is to "focus the knowledge, expertise, and leadership of our nation's educators on sustained efforts to improve writing and learning for all learners." Here is a link to its mission and core principles: www.nwp.org/cs/public/print/doc/about.csp.

Unofficially, of course, what it really does is provide a space where, like Camelot, "for one brief shining moment" (in this case, a Summer Institute) you can work with dedicated teachers in all content areas at all levels to learn how best to help students communicate their content. And in so doing, I believe another symptomatic shift will also occur. As we become better trained in interdisciplinary flexibility and become higher-quality teachers, our profession will grow in both its reputation and leadership.

The National Writing Project was started in the Bay Area and has grown to chapters all over the country where teachers of all disciplines learn how to apply writing to every content area. It's a summer program that will change your teaching forever, and it's a profession-changing, if not life-changing, experience.

In fact, according to research conducted by the NWP, since its founding as the Bay Area Writing Project in 1974, approximately 70,000 teachers have participated in an Invitational Summer Institute. Furthermore, annually, approximately 3,000 teachers participate in Invitational Summer Institutes all over the country, and

100,000 educators participate in other opportunities offered by local Writing Project sites. And these teachers come from all walks of life, all disciplines, and all grade levels.

In fact, just to break it down a little and show you the party you might be missing, the following data shows the diversity in those Summer Institutes. Of the teachers who participated as Fellows in 2010:

- Over 35 percent were elementary-level teachers teaching all content areas;
- Approximately 22 percent were middle school teachers;
- About 30 percent were high school teachers;
- 12 percent taught college and beyond.

That's a room of teachers unlike any other, learning from each other and learning together. And in terms of content areas, over the past ten years:

- Over 24 percent of the teachers who have gone through a branch of the National Writing Project are science teachers or are elementary-level teachers who teach science.
- Over 27 percent of the teachers teach math or are elementary-level teachers who also teach math.

And, according to an analysis of the Invitational Summer Institute survey, conducted by Inverness Research, looking at teachers' self-reported discipline:

- 11 percent of institute participants are single-subject teachers who specialize in mathematics, science, history/social science, foreign language, or art/music;
- 14 percent teach special education, bilingual education, or another non-discipline-specific area (such as a technology educator or librarian).

For more details about this study, go to: www.inverness-research.org/reports/2011-11-Rpt-NWP-NWP-Survey-TeacherInst-Final.pdf.

The program itself is unique, a celebration of the "teachers teaching teachers" paradigm. It is effective professional development, and that in itself can be unfortunately uncommon.

It's a program where the greatest educators and authors and presenters sit and share their craft with those teachers most willing to learn.

Just imagine a film school that selected its participants from a large pool of directing students, and allowed those students (say, twenty of them total) to spend a month of their summer in dialogue with the greatest directors of our time. During their summer, Spielberg would sit down for a day in their midst, bringing with him one of his greatest life and professional lessons to pass on for them to make their own. Scorsese would participate too, Spike Lee, and Spike Jonze. Can you just imagine the movies, the new cinematic treasures that would be born of such a summer?

Just imagine being a baseball player given the opportunity to spend a month in the company of Willie Mays, Sandy Koufax, and Yogi Berra. Can you imagine the brilliant plays and games of legend that would come out of such a season of learning?

So is it also true with the National Writing Project and its various branches all over the country. Every summer, in many cities in the United States, small cohorts of teachers, representing every grade level from pre-K through college level and any subject possible, gather together to participate in an NWP Summer Institute.

But their excitement only lasts so long before the mental sweat begins. Their hands cramp daily, their brains ache with the challenges asked, as authors, professors, journalists, and educators come before them to pass on their knowledge. The goal? To create writers from these groups of diverse teachers, the theory being that if we can teach teachers more about the craft of writing, their knowledge will slowly ripple out into their own staffs, improving both the quality of the teachers around them and the level of student achievement in all of their school sites.

You can tell a teacher is a Fellow of the Writing Project from the quality of product his or her students produce. You can see it in the 4Cs-focused projects the students create, in the level of voice in the students' work, in their risk-taking, and, most importantly, in their enjoyment of learning.

For one month each summer, in cities all over the United States, groups of teachers experience this amazing program, where they are granted the opportunity to work with other academically curious teachers, a mythical school staff of like-minded individuals, all on fire with their own learning and all looking towards the fall when they can spread that fire to their students. It is a unique staff, a faculty lounge of learning unlike any that they have worked with before.

If you are interested in discovering more about the National Writing Project, if you are interested in seeing some of what is produced by teachers and their students, or if you are interested in joining the national conversation of interdisciplinary writing as it relates to the Common Core, check out the National Writing Project website at http://digitalis.nwp.org.

You can join the discussion groups working together to discuss content-area literacy across the disciplines and this new world of Common Core Standards at http://connect.nwp.org/lcc.

The following books might also help you as you explore your next summer of professional possibility:

- Roni Jo Draper's book: *(Re)imagining Content Area Literacy*, www.nwp.org/cs/public/print/books/literacyinstruction.
- WAC Journal, *The WAC Journal: Research and Ideas in Writing Across the Curriculum*, www.nwp.org/cs/public/print/resource/3877.

Want to improve how you and your students can communicate your subject? Want to learn methods and strategies of communication in a room of teachers who are all united towards the goal of learning and improving their teaching? Want to address this new Common Core universal writing standard in a proactive way that allows your voice to be a voice of leadership in communication and interdisciplinary studies? Then spending your summer with your local branch of the National Writing Project is for you.

This is a call to action unlike any other. It is vital to learn how math, numbers, and logic apply to our world. For without math, how can we learn the patterns and predictions of the world around us? It is vital that we learn science and how our world works, at both a micro and macro level. For without science, how do we lead our species into the brave new world of the future? It is vital to learn history and the patterns of human interactions and creations. For without history, how do we advance as a civilization willing to learn from both our victories and our failures? PE is vital. Art is vital. Music is vital. Computer science is vital. And writing unites them all.

Get thee to a Writing Project. Promote your content by advancing your knowledge of how to best communicate that content. Learn to write, and in so doing, your ability and desire to see your students writing about your subject will grow. Soon after your knowledge grows, theirs will too.

Becoming a writer is an adventure. Becoming a writing teacher is the future. Good luck on your writing journey.

Appendix A: TED Persuasive/Memoir Unit

As you know, we have been looking at TED speeches on occasion this last quarter, and now it's time to put our knowledge to some use. These TED speeches are really a combination of different writing genres: literary analysis, research, argument, and memoir.

Goal: To write a TED-esque speech to perform for our classes.

Below is a rough checklist of assignments at which we will be chipping throughout the course of this unit. Be flexible. Some of these may fall by the wayside as we move through the unit together and other, smaller, gap-filling assignments may be added to enhance a particular concept.

We will be spending time in class chipping away at all of these assignments. However, finishing them by the deadlines is up to you, and outside work may be necessary to accomplish everything. Keep up on your deadlines, and don't leave things to the last minute.

Date Assigned	Assignment	Due Date
	Signed team charter	
	Research plan	
	Speech analysis blog post (submit online)	
	Problem statement	
	Infographic blog post analysis (submit online)	
	RadioLab episode analysis	
	Bibliography research check #1	
	How to link text mini-lesson	
	Bibliography research check #2	
	Website plan due (flow-chart, outline, web, etc.)	
	Infographic final draft	
	TED speech rough draft due	
	TED speech final draft due	
	PowerPoint, Prezi, etc., due (with infographic embedded within it)	
	"Four Tips for Giving a Great Speech" blog post (flipped: watch at home, discussion in class)	
	RadioLab segment due (five minute limit)	
	Advertising flyers for event	
	Website published (post link on class website)	
	Collaboration peer evaluation due	
	TED performance (ten minute limit)	

Appendix B: Student-Created Rubric (from 'Tween Crayons and Curfews)

Student-Created Persuasive Essay Rubric

ELA?	Score 5 ABLE TO TEACH	Score 4 IT GETS THERE	Score 3 NOT QUITE, TRY HARDER	Score 2 ARE YOU LISTENING?	Score 1 EPIC FAIL
Ideas (What thoughts went into it!)	• Great thesis statement that's a map of the essay. • Great evidence, quotes. • Great counterargument that says, "OK, I get that there are others who don't agree with me and WHY."	• Good thesis that says what you're going to prove. • Good evidence (quotes, personal experience). • Says there are people who don't agree, but don't give them a lot of time, space to explain WHY.	• Thesis is there, somewhere in the essay. • Only some evidence, but not for each point. • Only says in one line that there are those who disagree.	• What's this paper about? • No evidence (you didn't prove it). • Not one mention of people who disagree with you.	Can't read it, not a persuasive essay.
Organization (Can your reader follow it?)	• Really clear, like building blocks from one idea to another. • Bull's-eye every time! • Every piece of the prompt is included clearly.	• The reader can definitely follow the logic. • Generally stays on target. • The whole prompt is in there somewhere.	• Um, I think I get where you're going with this. • Drifts! • Tries to answer the prompt, but it's missing something.	• The reader doesn't follow you. • Blurry, like dirt on your glasses, unfocused. • Doesn't answer the prompt.	
Organization (Can your reader follow it?)	• Really high-level words! • Tons of sentence types and lengths (texture). • Great transitions (to quote, to commentary, between paragraphs). • Good use of paragraphs to divide ideas.	• Good, grade level vocabulary. • Some sentence variety. • A few transitions words or phrases here or there. • Uses multiple paragraphs.	• Simple vocab (good, happy, nice, fine, etc.). • Only one kind of sentence, and it gets boring in the rhythm. • Bumpy transitions! • Doesn't seem to understand why you need paragraphs.	• Repeats key words over and over. • Simple sentences. • No transitions (the reader must jump across gaps). • One LOOONNNGGGG paragraph.	
Conventions (Do your errors get in the way?)	• Only a couple of errors (like a really good rough draft).	• Some errors, but they don't get in the way of what the reader understands.	• Lots of errors, but the reader can still understand what you mean.	• What the heck did the author mean by that?!	

Reproduced with permission from Wolpert-Gawron (2011), 'Tween crayons and curfews: Tips for middle school teachers. Larchmont, NY: Eye On Education.

Appendix C: Oral Feedback Sheet

Resources: Assessment

Teacher Feedback

Project-Based Writing Connection: Getting one-on-one conference time with the teacher can help you focus on what you are doing right and what you need to work on.

At times, you might need help with some aspect of your project. Often, a quick conference with your teacher will do just the trick. Be prepared to make the most out of the opportunity to receive such helpful feedback.

Take the form below with you to your conference. Take notes as your teacher talks; this will help you absorb the information more fully. You can use these notes later as a reference when you are revising or finalizing your paper.

Teacher Note: You might not need to fill in every line of this form. Just use it as a guide.

Own Your Own Feedback

Notes on Your Topic/Theme: _____

_____

_____

Notes on Your Thesis Statement: _____

_____

_____

This is great: Keep doing it, don't change a thing! (List skills you've done well .)

_____

_____

This could be better: Reconsider, mull over, overhaul . (List items you still need to work on.)

_____

_____

Based on the work in front of me today, my teacher is giving me a(n) _____.

(enter grade)

Think about it: Am I satisfied with that grade?   Yes   No

Due date of final draft, based on our discussion: _____

Signed: _____   Date: _____

Courtesy of Teacher Created Resources: Oral Feedback Sheet

Appendix D: The Problem Statement

You are going to be developing what is called a "problem statement." In terms of college and career readiness, a problem statement is used anywhere from a doctorate thesis to a business proposal. It states the goal for your research and the problem you wish to solve. Ultimately, it is meant to help the focus the topic of your persuasive TED speech.

To create a problem statement, you must write a paragraph that includes the following information:

1. States the broad problem/topic about which you are interested in researching.
2. Defines the problem you will be solving by narrowing the issue.
3. Describes why it needs to be investigated by giving background information and context.
4. States your goals in writing and researching this problem (I will . . ., I plan . . ., I would like . . ., I propose . . ., etc.).

From there, you will develop three to five questions based on the problem statement. These specific questions will further serve to guide your writing. By answering them through your investigation, you should then more easily find a solution or answer to your problem, which will be a main focus of your persuasive speech.

Here is an example of a completed problem statement and five corresponding questions that are specific to our speech-writing assignment. Notice how the paragraph starts out broad in its scope and narrows down to a more specific goal:

> Bullying has long been a problem with children and adults alike. While bullying can be seen even in the workplace amongst adults, those who bully as grown-ups may also be those who bully as children. Children all over our country are victims of bullying, but bullying comes in many forms, some physical and some mental. We must combat this plague from many different angles in order to make bullies uncomfortable in their intimidation. I propose to write an argumentation speech that investigates the different forms of bullying and how we can band together to stop it.

Questions:
1. What are the forms of bullying?
2. What defines bullying?
3. Can a bully be reformed?
4. What are methods a victim can use to stop being bullied?
5. What can schools, the government, laws, families do to invest in solving this problem?

Appendix E: Narrative/Informational Writing Checklist

Throughout the course of this first quarter, we will be working towards the goal of refining our skills as narrative writers. We will also be working on building up our skills as writers of informational texts. To do so, we are using this checklist as a means to remain organized and on task. This checklist should be at school every day as sometimes things will be deleted, dates might adjust, or assignments may be added. I ask that you be flexible. Note: being flexible is far easier if you don't leave assignments to the last minute.

This unit honors the 4Cs: creativity, collaboration, critical thinking, and communication. That is, we will use all of these skills throughout the unit. This unit expects that you submit some assignments online, and some in class.

I have also included links as resources to help in your own independent learning. The expectation is that you are learning with me and despite me. You are learning with others and on your own. You are learning, but you are also teaching others. You are also expected to be your own advocate. Have questions? Freaking out? Talk to me. I'm your guide, and I'm here to help you achieve these goals to the best of your ability. I'm also here to push you to challenge what you think of as your best.

Attached is a rough checklist of assignments at which we will be chipping away throughout the course of this unit.

Good luck, and reach out to me anytime.
Mrs. Wolpert-Gawron

Assigned	Assignment	Due	Tardy?
	Inquiry chart Historical fiction Science fiction (Classwork)	In class	
	Select book (bring it in daily)—bring it in by this date for the easiest homework grade ever!		
	Finish book—use this date as a goal		
	Fan fiction analysis (homework to be submitted online)		
	Research check #1 Bibliography uses APA format (counts as a quiz!) http://owl.english.purdue.edu/owl/resource/560/01/ http://www.easybib.com/		
	Research check #2 Bibliography uses APA format (counts as a quiz!)		
	Google search story due https://searchstories-intl.appspot.com/en-us/ (send me the link by the end of the date given)		
	Choose Your Own Adventure analysis	In class	
	Commit to narrative format (fan fiction or *Choose Your Own Adventure*)		
	Pixar's Rules of Storytelling analysis http://i.imgur.com/DH1IF.jpg (blog post)		
	What if . . . the first astronauts had died? Speech analysis http://www.archives.gov/press/press-kits/american-originals-photos/moon-disaster-1.jpg (blog post)		
	Research plan	In class	
	Google advanced search screen shot due (email me the screen shot)		
	Linking text	In class	
	Rough draft narrative due (hard copy in class—typed with links indicated)		
	Final draft narrative due (use Dropbox folders)		
	What if . . .? PowerPoint/Prezi/Keynote due		
	What if . . .? Oral presentations		

Resources: Organization

The Writing-Genre Matrix

 Project-Based Writing Connection: This resource can get you thinking about the structure, purpose, and content of different forms of writing. This helps you choose the best genre(s) for your purpose when writing.

There are many similarities and differences between the writing genres, and knowing this can help you understand how all of the genres relate to one another.

Directions: Study the matrix below, which shows the various elements that go into four different genres of writing: Narrative, Persuasive, Summary, and Response to Literature .

Genre	Narrative a story/sequence of events	Persuasive a piece meant to convince	Summary a quick retelling	Response an analysis of a written piece
Hook				
Background Info				
Thesis Statement				
TAG (title/author/genre)				
Main Topic Sentence				
Evidence				
Commentary				
Transition Words				
Voice				
Sentence Variety				
Conventions				
Figurative Language				
Plot				
Rising Action				
Exposition				
Setting				
Characters				
Conflict				
Falling Action				
Resolution				
Theme				
Counterargument				
Call to Action/Solution				

Courtesy of Teacher Created Resources: Writing Genre Matrix

Appendix G: The DARPA Project Checklist

Due Date	Description	Completed	Tardy?
	Group delegation # and group name		
	Google account set up (invite me)		
	Science fiction narrative		
	Research check #1		
	Research check #2		
	Executive summary rough draft		
	Group poster		
	Blackboard collaborate: virtual classroom group check with me		
	Final draft executive summary (individual contribution)		
	Assembled final draft collaborative executive summary		
	Website due		
	Panel presentation		

Appendix H: Peer Review Packet (from *'Tween Crayons and Curfews*)

In a peer review packet, a student sits down with their peer, exchanges rough drafts, and fills out a review packet of activities that is based on the genre being written. For instance, the packet might include the following activities:

- Write another hook for their peer.
- Create a word splat of high-level words, a word bank created by a peer looking to identify great vocabulary. Keep a tally of the transition words or phrases the peer has used.
- Indicate where the thesis statement might be in need of help.
- Color-code different elements of the essay to visually display what might be missing from the paper.

By filling out the packet, not only is a student reading an essay in a very targeted way and commenting on it, but that student is also aware of how his peer might be responding to his own essay as well. In so doing, it makes a student aware of his own essay's needs when the student gets the paper back for formal revision.

By the way, the use of a peer review packet is universal.

- In math, a peer review packet can be created that breaks down the components of an equation, asking students to analyze different variables or a peer's process of achieving an answer. The stations could be very similar to those listed above in that they could help students answer lengthy analytical or word problems.
- In science, they could be used for lab work, breaking down the elements of the scientific method and verifying the accuracy of conclusions.
- In history, a student can have his history day project critiqued by a peer prior to finalizing it.
- In study skills, a station can focus on note-taking advice or binder organization.

Training these students to achieve as teachers gives them the highest-level communication skills ever. Additionally, there is also an awesome by-product. If you train them to be rigorous in their feedback of one another, they can be giving more individual attention to each other than you with your red pen ever could.

Reproduced with permission from Wolpert-Gawron (2011), *'Tween Crayons and Curfews: Tips for Middle School Teachers*. Larchmont, NY: Eye On Education.

Getting a Reader's Attention

 Project-Based Writing Connection: When adding a written component to your project, use a hook to grab your reader's attention right from the start.

A hook is that first moment of a paper—be it a narrative or an essay—that catches the reader's attention and makes him or her want to read more.

Here is a list of hooks using different strategies to begin the same essay: a piece written about the lost colony of Roanoke. As you can see, there are many ways to hook a reader.

Definition	**Onomatopoeia**
A colony is defined as a group of people who leave their native land to settle in a land with the intent on remaining connected to its original country.	Scratch. Scritch. The settler quickly etched the mysterious message into the tree never to know if it was going to be seen by another human.
Dialogue	**Simile/Metaphor**
"Where are they all?" the first mate whispered, chills covering the sailors as they each thought about the disappearance of the people who should have been there to greet them.	When Capt. John White landed back in Roanoke in 1590, he was greeted with a mystery as deep as the sea on which he had sailed.
Fact/Statistic	**Staccato Three-Word Lead**
In the late 16th Century, 110 men, women, and children made the brave journey to the New World.	Men. Women. Children. They all disappeared without a trace, leaving us to solve the mystery of their whereabouts.
In the Middle of the Action	**Theme**
As the ship dropped anchor and the vessel slowly glided to a halt, the men, women, and children all gathered on the deck for a first look at their new home.	Traveling to the New World was dangerous, but the people of Roanoke left us a mystery of those dangers that would haunt historians for years to come.

Directions: After reading each of these examples, think of an essay you are working on. You may be revising or just beginning. Try to start the piece of writing using each of these strategies. Then, pass your new list of hooks to your classmate or to an adult family member. Have him or her circle the three he or she feels are the strongest. Pick one of these three hooks to use when writing or revising.

Bibliography

Applebee, Arthur. "Great Writing Comes Out of Great Ideas." *The Atlantic*. N.p., 27 Sept. 2012. Web. 02 June 2013. http://www.theatlantic.com/national/archive/2012/09/great-writing-comes-out-of-great-ideas/262653/

"Articles for Educators." *POWERS: Pre-writing, Organize, Write, Edit, Revise, Share*. N.p., n.d. Web. 03 June 2013. http://www.articlesforeducators.com/article.asp?aid=106

"AVID | Decades of College Dreams." *AVID | Decades of College Dreams*. N.p., n.d. Web. 03 June 2013. http://www.avid.org/

Blau, S. (June 2007). The University of California Irvine Writing Project, Irvine, CA.

Boettcher, Judith V. and Rita-Marie Conrad. *The Online Teaching Survival Guide: Simple and Practical Pedagogical Tips*. San Francisco: Jossey-Bass, 2010. Print.

"CHARTER SCHOOLS Additional Federal Attention Needed to Help Protect Access for Students with Disabilities." *EdWeek Blogs*. United States Government Accountability Office, June 2012. Web. http://democrats.edworkforce.house.gov/sites/democrats.ed workforce.house.gov/files/documents/112/pdf/letters/Charter%20School%20SWD%20full %20report_%20June%202012.pdf

Cleaver, Samantha. "A Parent's Guide to the Common Core Standards." *Education.com*. N.p., n.d. Web. 03 June 2013. http://www.education.com/magazine/article/parents-guide-to-common-core-standards/

Coats, Emma. "Pixar's 22 Rules of Storytelling." Cartoon. N.p., n.d. Web. http://i.imgur.com/DH1lF.jpg

Culham, Ruth. "The Trait Lady Speaks Up." *Educational Leadership* 64.2 (2006): 53–7; and *Academic Search Premier*. 4 March 2007.

Daniels, Harvey, Steven Zemelman, and Nancy Steineke. *Content-Area Writing: Every Teacher's Guide*. Portsmouth, NH: Heinemann, 2007. Print.

Davis, Lauren. *The 5 Things Every Teacher Should Be Doing to Meet the Common Core State Standards*. Issue brief. Larchmont: Eye On Education, 2012. Print.

Fazio, Xavier and Tiffany Gallagher. "Supporting Students' Writing in Elementary Science: Tools to Facilitate Revision of Inquiry-Based Compositions." Diss. UC Davis, 2009. *Supporting Students' Writing in Elementary Science: Tools to Facilitate Revision of Inquiry-Based*

Compositions. Web. http://ejlts.ucdavis.edu/article/2009/8/4/supporting-students%E2%80%99-writing-elementary-science-tools-facilitate-revision-inquiry-b

Friedrich, L. (2011). Personal correspondence.

Gallagher, Kelly. *Write like This: Teaching Real-World Writing through Modeling & Mentor Texts*. Portland, ME: Stenhouse, 2011. Print.

The George Lucas Educational Foundation. (2012). www.edutopia.com

Hanks, T. (May, 2005). "The Power of Four." Vassar College Graduation Day Speech. Poughkeepsie, NY.

Harrington, L. (2012). Personal correspondence.

Hillocks, George. *Teaching Argument Writing, Grades 6–12: Supporting Claims with Relevant Evidence and Clear Reasoning*. Portsmouth, NH: Heinemann, 2011. Print.

"International Networks Archive / Map of the Month." *International Networks Archive / Map of the Month*. N.p., n.d. Web. 03 June 2013. http://www.princeton.edu/~ina/infographics/starbucks.html

"Jane Schaffer Writing Program." *Jane Schaffer Writing Program*. N.p., n.d. Web. 03 June 2013. http://www.janeschaffer.com/

Kuszewski, Andrea. "The Educational Value of Creative Disobedience." *The Creativity Post*. N.p., 23 June 2012. Web. 02 June 2013. http://blogs.scientificamerican.com/guest-blog/2011/07/07/the-educational-value-of-creative-disobedience/

"Lance Armstrong." *Lance Armstrong*. N.p., n.d. Web. 03 June 2013. http://www.lancearmstrong.com/

Larson, Sherri. "Multigenre Writing: An Answer to Many Questions." *Minnesota English Journal* (n.d.): 180–95. Web. http://www.mcte.org/journal/mej08/Larson.pdf

Lica, S. (2012). Personal correspondence.

"The Logic of Scientific Arguments." *Understanding Science*. N.p., n.d. Web. 02 June 2013. http://undsci.berkeley.edu/article/howscienceworks_07

Menerey, S. (2012). Personal correspondence.

Mercer, A. (2011). Personal correspondence.

"Mission Statement." *Common Core State Standards Initiative*. Common Core State Standards Initiative, 2012. Web. 02 June 2013. http://www.corestandards.org/

"National Archives and Records Administration." *National Archives and Records Administration*. N.p., n.d. Web. 03 June 2013. http://www.archives.gov/

"National Writing Project." *National Writing Project*. N.p., n.d. Web. 02 June 2013. http://www.nwp.org/

"The Partnership for 21st Century Skills." *The Partnership for 21st Century Skills*. N.p., n.d. Web. 02 June 2013. http://www.p21.org/

Peha, Steve. "Welcome to Teaching That Makes Sense!" *Teaching That Makes Sense!* N.p., n.d. Web. 03 June 2013. http://www.ttms.org/

"Percentage of Gifted and Talented Students in Public Elementary and Secondary Schools, by Sex, Race/Ethnicity, and State: 2004 and 2006." *Percentage of Gifted and Talented Students in Public Elementary and Secondary Schools, by Sex, Race/Ethnicity, and State: 2004 and 2006.* National Center for Education Statistics, n.d. Web. 02 June 2013. http://nces.ed.gov/programs/digest/d10/tables/dt10_049.asp

"Piktochart: Infographic and Presentation Tool for Non-Designers | Infographics | Best Info Graphic Design." *Piktochart Infographics.* N.p., n.d. Web. 03 June 2013. http://piktochart.com/?gclid=CMKuiMTt2LkCFZFcQgodAV0AgQ

Powell, R. (2011). Personal correspondence.

Ratzel, M. (2011). Personal correspondence.

"ReadWriteThink." *Readwritethink.org.* N.p., n.d. Web. 03 June 2013.

"Response: Using Ed Tech to Create 'Deep & Meaningful Experiences'" *Classroom Q & A with Larry Ferlazzo.* EdWeek, 19 Dec. 2012. Web. http://blogs.edweek.org/teachers/classroom_qa_with_larry_ferlazzo/2012/12/response_using_ed_tech_to_create_deep_meaningful_experiences.html

Robelen, Erik. "Man vs. Computer: Who Wins the Essay-Scoring Challenge?" *Education Week.* N.p., n.d. Web. 02 June 2013. http://blogs.edweek.org/edweek/curriculum/2012/04/computer_v_human_who_wins_the.html

Romano, Tom. *Blending Genre, Altering Style.* N.p.: Heinemann, 2000. Print.

"The Standards." *Common Core State Standards Initiative.* Common Core State Standards Initiative, 2012. Web. 02 June 2013. . http://www.corestandards.org/

Stokes, Laura. "The Enduring Quality and Value of the National Writing Project's Teacher Development Institutes: Teachers' Assessments of NWP Contributions to Their Classroom Practice and Development as Leaders." *Inverness-research.org.* N.p., Nov. 2011. Web.

TED: Ideas Worth Spreading. (2012). Retrieved from www.TED.com.

Unrau, Norman. *Content Area Reading and Writing: Fostering Literacies in Middle and High School Cultures.* Upper Saddle River, NJ: Pearson/Merrill/Prentice Hall, 2004. Print.

USA. NYC.gov. Department of Education. *Project-Based Learning: Inspiring Middle School Students to Engage in Deep and Active Learning.* NYC Department of Education, 2009. Web. http://schools.nyc.gov/documents/teachandlearn/project_basedfinal.pdf

Washburne, Carleton W. "Adjusting the Program to the Child." *Educational Leadership* (1953): 138–47. *ASCD.org.* Web.

"Welcome to the Purdue OWL." *Purdue OWL: APA Formatting and Style Guide.* N.p., n.d. Web. 03 June 2013. http://owl.english.purdue.edu/owl/resource/560/18/

Winters, Marcus A. and Jay P. Greene, "Civic Report 58 | How Special Ed Vouchers Keep Kids From Being Mislabeled as Disabled." *Civic Report 58 | How Special Ed Vouchers Keep Kids From Being Mislabeled as Disabled.* Manhattan Institute for Policy Research, 8 Aug. 2009. Web. 02 June 2013. http://www.manhattan-institute.org/html/cr_58.htm

Wolpert-Gawron, Heather. *'Tween Crayons and Curfews: Tips for Middle School Teachers.* Larchmont: Eye On Education, 2011. Print.

Wolpert-Gawron, Heather. *Project Based Writing*. Westminster: Teacher Created Resources, 2014. Print.

"Writing an Argumentative Essay." *Writing an Argumentative Essay*. N.p., n.d. Web. 02 June 2013. http://www.buowl.boun.edu.tr/students/types%20of%20essays/argumentative/ARGUM ENTATIVE.htm

Zinsser, William. *Writing to Learn: How to Write and Think Clearly about Any Subject at All*. New York: Harper & Row, 1988. Print.